www.wadsworth.com

wadsworth.com is the World Wide Web site for Thomson Wadsworth and is your direct source to dozens of online resources.

At *wadsworth.com* you can find out about supplements, demonstration software, and student resources. You can also send email to many of our authors and preview new publications and exciting new technologies.

wadsworth.com
Changing the way the world learns®

MUSIC
for
EAR TRAINING

CD-ROM and Workbook

SECOND EDITION

Michael Horvit   Timothy Koozin   Robert Nelson

Moores School of Music, University of Houston

Software production team

Timothy Rolls

Jill Bays-Purtill

Kristine Woldy

Timothy Nord

Shanta Sivasingham

Crystal Visco

Software design

Timothy Koozin

SCHIRMER

THOMSON LEARNING

Australia • Canada • Mexico • Singapore • Spain
United Kingdom • United States

SCHIRMER

THOMSON LEARNING

Music Editor: Clark Baxter
Senior Development Editor: Sharon Adams Poore
Senior Assistant Editor: Julie Yardley
Editorial Assistant: Anne Gittinger
Technology Project Manager: Michelle Vardeman
Marketing Manager: Diane Wenckebach
Marketing Assistant: Rachel Bairstow
Advertising Project Manager: Kelley McAllister

Project Manager, Editorial Production: Mary Noel
Print/Media Buyer: Rebecca Cross
Permissions Editor: Kiely Sexton
Production Service: Stratford Publishing Services, Inc.
Cover Designer: Bill Reuter, Reuter Design
Cover Image: Punchstock
Compositor: Stratford Publishing Services, Inc.
Printer: Quebecor World/Dubuque

For more information about our products, contact us at:
Thomson Learning Academic Resource Center
1-800-423-0563

For permission to use material from this text or product, submit a request online at http://www.thomsonrights.com.

Any additional questions about permissions can be submitted by email to thomsonrights@thomson.com.

Library of Congress Control Number: 2004107574

Student Edition: ISBN 0-534-62766-8

Annotated Instructor's Edition: ISBN 0-534-62767-6

Thomson Schirmer
10 Davis Drive
Belmont, CA 94002-3098
USA

Asia
Thomson Learning
5 Shenton Way #01-01
UIC Building
Singapore 068808

Australia/New Zealand
Thomson Learning
102 Dodds Street
Southbank, Victoria 3006
Australia

Canada
Nelson
1120 Birchmount Road
Toronto, Ontario M1K 5G4
Canada

Europe/Middle East/Africa
Thomson Learning
High Holborn House
50/51 Bedford Row
London WC1R 4LR
United Kingdom

Latin America
Thomson Learning
Seneca, 53
Colonia Polanco
11560 Mexico D.F.
Mexico

Spain/Portugal
Paraninfo
Calle Magallanes, 25
28015 Madrid, Spain

Contents ━━━━━━━━━━━━

Suggestions to the Student

Getting Started

UNIT 1   1

Intervals, Triads, and Scales   1

Major and minor seconds:	Quiz No. 1	1
	Quiz No. 2	2
Major and minor thirds:	Quiz No. 1	3
	Quiz No. 2	4
Perfect and augmented fourths:	Quiz No. 1	5
	Quiz No. 2	6
Perfect and diminished fifths:	Quiz No. 1	7
	Quiz No. 2	8
All perfect intervals and tritones:	Quiz No. 1	9
	Quiz No. 2	10
Major and minor sixths:	Quiz No. 1	11
	Quiz No. 2	12
Major and minor sevenths:	Quiz No. 1	13
	Quiz No. 2	14
All intervals:	Quiz No. 1	15
	Quiz No. 2	16
Major and minor triads:	Quiz No. 1	17
	Quiz No. 2	18
Introducing diminished triads:	Quiz No. 1	19
	Quiz No. 2	20
Introducing augmented triads:	Quiz No. 1	21
	Quiz No. 2	22
Major and minor scales:	Quiz No. 1	23
	Quiz No. 2	24

UNIT 2   25

Rhythmic Dictation: Simple meters   25

Rhythmic Dictation: Quiz No. 1   29
                               Quiz No. 2   30
                               Quiz No. 3   31

Melodic Dictation: Seconds, thirds, and fourths   32

Preliminary Exercises   32
Melodies   35
Melodic Dictation: Quiz No. 1   38
                               Quiz No. 2   39
                               Quiz No. 3   40

UNIT 3   41

Melodic Dictation: Fifths, sixths, and octaves   41

Preliminary Exercises   41
Melodies   44
Melodic Dictation: Quiz No. 1   47
                               Quiz No. 2   48
                               Quiz No. 3   50

Harmonic Dictation: Four part settings of the tonic triad   52

Harmonic Dictation   Quiz No. 1   54
                               Quiz No. 2   55
                               Quiz No. 3   56

UNIT 4   57

Rhythmic Dictation: Beat subdivision by 2   57

Rhythmic Dictation: Quiz No. 1   60
                               Quiz No. 2   61
                               Quiz No. 3   62

Melodic Dictation: The tonic triad and dominant seventh   63

Preliminary Exercises   63
Melodies   65
Melodic Dictation: Quiz No. 1   69
                               Quiz No. 2   71
                               Quiz No. 3   72

Harmonic Dictation: The tonic triad and dominant seventh   74

Basic Progressions   74
Phrase-length Exercises   83
Harmonic Dictation: Quiz No. 1   86
                               Quiz No. 2   87
                               Quiz No. 3   88

UNIT 5   89

Rhythmic Dictation: Beat subdivision by 4; Anacrusis   89

    Rhythmic Dictation: Quiz No. 1   92
                                                            Quiz No. 2   93
                                                              Quiz No. 3   95

Melodic Dictation: Primary triads and the dominant seventh   97

    Preliminary Exercises   97
    Melodies   98
    Melodic Dictation: Quiz No. 1   102
                                                              Quiz No. 2   104
                                                              Quiz No. 3   105

Harmonic Dictation: Primary triads and the dominant seventh; Cadential tonic six-four   107

    Basic Progressions   107
        Primary triads and the dominant seventh   107
        Cadential tonic six-four   109
    Phrase-length Exercises   111
    Harmonic Dictation: Quiz No. 1   114
                                                                 Quiz No. 2   115
                                                              Quiz No. 3   116

UNIT 6   117

Rhythmic Dictation: Dots and ties   117

    Rhythmic Dictation: Quiz No. 1   120
                                                            Quiz No. 2   121
                                                             Quiz No. 3   123

Melodic Dictation: Minor mode   125

    Preliminary Exercises   125
    Melodies   126
    Melodic Dictation: Quiz No. 1   130
                                                             Quiz No. 2   132
                                                             Quiz No. 3   134

Harmonic Dictation: Minor mode; First inversion of triads   136

    Basic Progressions   136
        Minor mode   136
        First inversion of triads   137
    Phrase-length Exercises   140
    Harmonic Dictation: Quiz No. 1   144
                                                                 Quiz No. 2   145
                                                              Quiz No. 3   147

UNIT 7   149

Melodic Dictation: The supertonic triad   149

    Preliminary Exercises   149

Contents

    Melodies   150

    Melodic Dictation: Quiz No. 1   154

                                                Quiz No. 2   155

                                                Quiz No. 3   157

Harmonic Dictation: The supertonic triad; Inversions of V7   159

    Basic Progressions   159
        Supertonic triad   159
        Inversions of V7   161
    Phrase-length Exercises   163
    Harmonic Dictation: Quiz No. 1   166

                                                Quiz No. 2   168

                                                Quiz No. 3   170

UNIT 8   172

Rhythmic Dictation: Compound meter   172

    Rhythmic Dictation: Quiz No. 1   175

                                                  Quiz No. 2   176

                                                Quiz No. 3   177

Melodic Dictation: All diatonic triads   178

    Preliminary Exercises   178
    Melodies   180
    Melodic Dictation: Quiz No. 1   183

                                                Quiz No. 2   185

                                                Quiz No. 3   187

Harmonic Dictation: All diatonic triads   189

    Basic Progressions   189
    Phrase-length Exercises   194
    Harmonic Dictation: Quiz No. 1   197

                                                Quiz No. 2   198

                                                Quiz No. 3   200

UNIT 9   202

Rhythmic Dictation: Triplets   202

    Rhythmic Dictation: Quiz No. 1   205

                                                  Quiz No. 2   206

                                                Quiz No. 3   207

Melodic Dictation: Supertonic and leading tone sevenths   208

    Preliminary Exercises   208
    Melodies   209
    Melodic Dictation: Quiz No. 1   214

                                                Quiz No. 2   215

                                                Quiz No. 3   217

Harmonic Dictation: Supertonic and leading tone sevenths   219

Basic Progressions   219
Phrase-length Exercises   224
Harmonic Dictation: Quiz No. 1   228
                                       Quiz No. 2   230
                                       Quiz No. 3   232

UNIT 10   234

Examples from Music Literature   234

    1. Johann Sebastian Bach   Minuet in G   234

    2. Johann Sebastian Bach   *Aus meines Herzens Grunde* (chorale)   235

    3. Johann Sebastian Bach   *Wir glauben all' an einen Gott* (chorale)   235

    4. Ludwig van Beethoven   Six Variations on *Nel cor più non mi sento*   236

    5. Friedrich Kuhlau   Sonatina Op. 88, No. 3, mvt. III   236

    6. Wolfgang Amadeus Mozart   String Quintet, K. 581, mvt. IV   237

Quiz No. 1   238
    Joseph Haydn   Sonata in D Major, Hob. XVI:33, Menuetto con Variazioni   238

Quiz No. 2   239
    John Farmer   *Fair Phyllis* (chorale)   239

Quiz No. 3   240
    Wolfgang Amadeus Mozart   String Quartet, K. 80, mvt. III, Trio   240

UNIT 11   241

Rhythmic Dictation: Syncopation   241

    Rhythmic Dictation: Quiz No. 1   244
                                       Quiz No. 2   245
                                       Quiz No. 3   247

Melodic Dictation: Non-dominant seventh chords   248

    Preliminary Exercises   248
    Melodies   249
    Melodic Dictation: Quiz No. 1   253
                                       Quiz No. 2   254
                                       Quiz No. 3   256

Harmonic Dictation: Non-dominant seventh chords   258

    Basic Progressions   258
    Phrase-length Exercises   261
    Harmonic Dictation: Quiz No. 1   264
                                       Quiz No. 2   266
                                       Quiz No. 3   268

UNIT 12   270

Melodic Dictation: Scalar variants, modal borrowing, and decorative chromaticism   270

Preliminary Exercises   270

    Scalar variants   270

    Modal borrowing   271

    Decorative chromaticism   273

Melodies   276

Melodic Dictation: Quiz No. 1   280

                                      Quiz No. 2   282

                                      Quiz No. 3   284

Harmonic Dictation: Scalar variants; Modal borrowing   285

Basic Progressions   285

    Scalar variants   285

    Modal borrowing   287

Phrase-length Exercises   290

Harmonic Dictation: Quiz No. 1   295

                                      Quiz No. 2   297

                                      Quiz No. 3   299

UNIT 13   301

Melodic Dictation: Secondary dominants   301

Preliminary Exercises   301

Melodies   303

Melodic Dictation: Quiz No. 1   307

                                      Quiz No. 2   308

                                      Quiz No. 3   310

Harmonic Dictation: Secondary dominants   312

Basic Progressions   312

Phrase-length Exercises   315

Harmonic Dictation: Quiz No. 1   319

                                      Quiz No. 2   321

                                      Quiz No. 3   323

UNIT 14   325

Examples from Music Literature   325

   1. Johann Sebastian Bach   *Herr, wie du willst, so shick's mit mir* (chorale)   325

   2. Johann Sebastian Bach   *Jesu, meiner Seelen Wonne* (chorale)   325

   3. Johann Sebastian Bach   *Wer nur den lieben Gott lässt walten* (chorale)   325

   4. Johann Sebastian Bach   Minuet in G Minor   326

   5. Edward MacDowell   *To a Wild Rose*, Op. 51, No. 1   326

   6. Carl Maria von Weber   German Dance   327

   7. Frederic Chopin   Valse, Op. 69, No. 1   327

   8. Wolfgang Amadeus Mozart   String Quartet, K. 158, mvt. I   328

   9. Joseph Haydn   Divertimento in D   329

10. Ludwig van Beethoven String Quartet, Op. 18, No. 6, mvt. I 330

Quiz No. 1 331
Johann Sebastian Bach *Jesu, meiner Seelen Wonne* (chorale) 331
Es woll'uns Gott genadig sein (chorale) 331

Quiz No. 2 332
Ludwig van Beethoven *Romanze* from Sonatina in G 332
Frederic Chopin Prelude, Op. 28, No. 7 332

Quiz No. 3 333
Joseph Haydn Divertimento in G, Hob. II:3 333

UNIT 15 334

Melodic Dictation: Modulation to closely related keys 334

Melodies 334
Melodic Dictation: Quiz No. 1 339
Quiz No. 2 340
Quiz No. 3 342

Harmonic Dictation: Modulation to closely related keys 343

Phrase-length Exercises 343
Harmonic Dictation: Quiz No. 1 348
Quiz No. 2 350
Quiz No. 3 352

UNIT 16 354

Rhythmic Dictation: Quintuple meter 354

Preliminary Exercises 354
Comprehensive Exercises 355
Rhythmic Dictation: Quiz No. 1 358
Quiz No. 2 359
Quiz No. 3 361

Melodic Dictation: The Neapolitan sixth chord, augmented sixth chords, and modulation to
distantly related keys 362

Preliminary Exercises 362
Melodies 364
Melodic Dictation: Quiz No. 1 368
Quiz No. 2 370
Quiz No. 3 372

Harmonic Dictation: The Neapolitan sixth chord, augmented sixth chords, enharmonic modulation 374

Basic Progressions 374
Phrase-length Exercises 377
Harmonic Dictation: Quiz No. 1 381
Quiz No. 2 383
Quiz No. 3 385

UNIT 17   387

Examples from Music Literature   387

    1. Johann Sebastian Bach   *Ach Gott, vom Himmel sieh' darein* (chorale)   387

    2. Johann Sebastian Bach   *Befiehl du deine Wege* (chorale)   387

    3. Johann Sebastian Bach   *Ach Gott, wie manches Herzeleid* (chorale)   388

    4. Johann Sebastian Bach   *Hilf, Herr Jesu, lass gelingen* (chorale)   389

    5. Johann Sebastian Bach   Bourrée, French Overture   390

    6. Jeremiah Clarke   Jigg   391

    7. Antonio Diabelli   Rondino   392

    8. Joseph Haydn   Sonata, Hob. XVI:27, mvt. III   392

    9. Ludwig van Beethoven   Bagatelle, Op. 119, No. 1   393

    10. Ludwig van Beethoven   Minuet in G Major, WoO 10, No. 2   393

    11. Mikail Ivanovich Glinka   Waltz, Op. 39, No. 15   394

    12. Franz Schubert   Scherzo in B-flat   394

    13. Joseph Haydn   Divertimento, Hob II:18, mvt. III, Trio   395

    14. Ludwig van Beethoven   Quartet, Op. 18, No. 1, mvt. III   396

    15. Ludwig van Beethoven   Quartet, Op. 18, No. 4, mvt. III   397

    16. Ludwig van Beethoven   Quartet, Op. 18, No. 4, mvt. IV   398

    17. Wolfgang Amadeus Mozart   Quartet, K. 421, mvt. III   399

    18. Wolfgang Amadeus Mozart   Quartet, K. 170, mvt. I   400

Quiz No. 1   402

    Johann Sebastian Bach   *Befiehl du deine Wege* (chorale)   402

    Domenico Scarlatti   Sonata, Longo 83   402

    Joseph Haydn   Sonata, Hob. XVI:37, mvt. III   403

    Ludwig van Beethoven   Sonata "Pathetique," Op. 13, mvt. III   403

Quiz No. 2   404

    Johann Sebastian Bach   *Meine Seel' erhebt den Herren* (chorale)   404

    Ludwig van Beethoven   Sonata, Op. 14, No. 1, mvt. II   405

    Johannes Brahms   Waltz, Op. 39, No. 15   405

    Ludwig van Beethoven   Quartet, Op. 18, No. 2, mvt. III, Trio   406

Quiz No. 3   407

    Johann Sebastian Bach   *Jesu, meine Freude* (chorale)   407

    Robert Schumann   "Important Event," *Scenes from Childhood*, Op. 15, No. 6   408

    Edvard Grieg   Rigaudon, Op. 40, No. 5, Trio   408

    Ludwig van Beethoven   Quartet, Op. 18, No. 3, mvt. III   409

UNIT 18   410

Rhythmic Dictation: Irregular meters   410

    Rhythmic Dictation: Quiz No. 1   413

                                 Quiz No. 2   414

Contents

Melodic Dictation: Diatonic modes   415

    Melodic Dictation: Quiz No. 1   419
                              Quiz No. 2   421

Harmonic Dictation: Diatonic modes   422

    Harmonic Dictation: Quiz No. 1   426
                              Quiz No. 2   428

UNIT 19   430

Rhythmic Dictation: Changing meters   430

    Rhythmic Dictation: Quiz No. 1   433
                              Quiz No. 2   434

Part Music Dictation: Pandiatonicism   435

    Part Music Dictation: Quiz No. 1   443
                              Quiz No. 2   446

UNIT 20   448

Rhythmic Dictation: Syncopation including irregular and mixed meters   448

    Rhythmic Dictation: Quiz No. 1   451
                              Quiz No. 2   452

Melodic Dictation: Extended and altered tertian harmony   454

    Melodic Dictation: Quiz No. 1   458
                              Quiz No. 2   460

Harmonic Dictation: Extended and altered tertian harmony   462

    Harmonic Dictation: Quiz No. 1   466
                              Quiz No. 2   468

UNIT 21   470

Melodic Dictation: Exotic scales   470

    Melodic Dictation: Quiz No. 1   475
                              Quiz No. 2   476

Part Music Dictation: Exotic scales   478

    Part Music Dictation: Quiz No. 1   482
                              Quiz No. 2   484

UNIT 22   485

Melodic Dictation: Quartal harmony   485

    Melodic Dictation: Quiz No. 1   489
                              Quiz No. 2   491

Part Music Dictation: Quartal harmony   493

    Part Music Dictation: Quiz No. 1   496
                              Quiz No. 2   498

UNIT 23   500

Part Music Dictation: Polyharmony and polytonality   500

    Part Music Dictation: Quiz No. 1   507
                                                    Quiz No. 2   510

UNIT 24   513

Melodic Dictation: Interval music   513

    Preliminary Exercises   513
    Melodies   516
    Melodic Dictation: Quiz No. 1   520
                                                  Quiz No. 2   522

UNIT 25   524

Melodic Dictation: Serial music   524

    Melodic Dictation: Quiz No. 1   528
                                                  Quiz No. 2   529

What's new in Version 2.0 of the CD-ROM

- Eight new units with 360 melodic, harmonic, and rhythmic dictation exercises provide graded study in post-tonal and jazz idioms.

- The newly designed interface is optimized for newer computer systems, including Macintosh OS X and Windows XP.

Suggestions to the Student

The ability to hear and quickly comprehend any piece of music is a skill that is crucial to the musician. Having a "good ear" involves more than just playing or singing in tune. Traditionally, students acquire this skill through the discipline of aural dictation—listening to a musical example and then writing it down. Unfortunately, all too many students approach this facet of their musical studies with trepidation and anxiety. They may assume that only those musicians blessed with perfect pitch can do dictation. In fact, aural comprehension is a skill that can be acquired with diligent, structured practice. The exercises on this CD-ROM are designed to give the student an ample number of ear-training practice exercises that can be completed outside the classroom and at the student's own pace. The exercises are carefully graded to lead from simple isolated problems, such as interval recognition, all the way to the transcription of short pieces from the literature. You can select from a variety of sonorities. You can listen to each exercise as often as you wish and choose various tempos. You can compare your results with the correct solution by clicking on the "**Show Answer**" button.

Four categories of exercises appear throughout the CD-ROM and Workbook:

- rhythmic dictation drills

- preliminary exercises for melodic dictation, which focus on particular musical patterns, and harmonic dictation, which focus on chord progressions

- melodies and phrase-length harmonic exercises

- and music from the literature.

Exercises in interval, triad, and scale recognition are contained in the first unit. You can return to this unit for review at any time. As a rule, the preliminary exercises introduce a specific item, such as an interval or a chord, and help you to assimilate that item through drill. The melodies and phrase-length harmonic exercises are cumulative and serve to integrate the new items into the vocabulary previously presented. The CD-ROM allows you to go back and review the interval and triad recognition drills from Unit 1 at any time. The units containing music from the literature will help you to gauge your progress. You will see how facility with the rhythmic, melodic, and harmonic exercises improves your understanding of the music that is the stuff of your day-to-day activities.

The CD-ROM also contains the quizzes that appear in each unit of the Workbook. These quizzes may be given in class or assigned as homework; your instructor may ask you to submit them. The solutions for these quizzes will not be found on the CD-ROM.

Since aural dictation is often a new experience, it is easy to become overwhelmed. Here are some general strategies that will help you to focus your listening and correctly interpret what you hear. These lists are not intended to exhaust all the possibilities; your instructor will likely have additional suggestions, and you will discover other useful devices on your own. From time to time, additional suggestions will appear on the screen. These suggestions are intended to help you deal with a particular exercise, but make a note of them, because they will come in handy for other exercises as well.

Rudiments

Unit 1 contains exercises for intervals, triads, and scales. In each category, Practice Drills offer a virtually unlimited number of problems. For intervals, you may elect to concentrate on just one size—say seconds—or you may elect to listen to as broad a range of sizes as you wish. There are similar options with triads and scales. Unit 1 is a valuable resource unit, and you should use it for review at any time. For example, the melodic dictation exercises are graded by interval content. You may wish to review the particular intervals before working on the melodies. Similarly, when seventh chords are introduced you might wish to review sevenths.

Rhythmic Dictation

1. Define the time signature (how many beats per measure, simple or compound, and so on), and then listen to the complete exercise.

2. How is the meter defined? Do you hear long notes on strong beats and quicker notes on weak beats? Try tapping the beat as you listen to the example.

3. What is the most frequently occurring note value? Is it the beat unit or a division of the beat? How many different values are there?

4. Do you hear recurring patterns? Are there instances of any particular rhythmic device such as syncopation?

Melodic Dictation

1. Listen to the complete exercise.

2. Establish the key for yourself by listening to either the given scale or the tonic note. (Simply click on the buttons for the scale or the note.)

3. Does the music move by step or by skip? Are the skips large or small? Do consecutive skips arpeggiate a particular chord?

4. What is the shape, or curve, of the melody? It can be helpful to draw a simple graph of its design before writing down the actual pitches.

5. Listen for important structural pitches. These include the first and last pitches, cadential pitches, metric and agogic accents, and the highest and lowest pitches. Try sketching in these pitches first.

6. Listen for phrase and cadence structure. What is the form of the melody? Are there interior cadences? Do two phrases form a period? Remember to constantly apply what you have learned in your theory classes. The more you are aware of what is likely to be true, the more you will hear.

   - Do you hear a pattern in the music? This patterning may be rhythmic only, or it may involve both rhythm and pitch. Are patterns repeated or sequenced? Are there recurrences of musical ideas, particularly at the beginning of subsequent phrases?

   - As you listen to a melody, sketch simple symbols to indicate pitches and rhythms; that is, circles for whole and half notes and dots for shorter note values. Allow for proportional distances between note heads to represent values within a measure. Supply precise rhythmic values as a subsequent step, then notate what you hear in final form.

   - An excellent method of enhancing your ability to take melodic dictation is to write down melodies from memory. When taking a break in the practice room or library, think of a tune you already know. It may be a folk, children's, popular, or patriotic song. Pick a key and jot it down. This will strengthen your ability to get material you clearly have in your mind down on paper.

Harmonic Dictation

1. Listen to the complete exercise.

2. For phrase-length exercises, what kind of cadence(s) do you hear?

3. Chord progressions in the common-practice period follow very predictable patterns. If you have identified one chord, consider the finite number of possibilities for chords that might logically follow. If you have identified the cadential chords, try working backwards.

4. The CD-ROM lets you isolate the individual voices. Hearing the lines clearly will help in distinguishing between two chords that are somewhat interchangeable, such as IV and ii6.

Examples from Music Literature

These exercises present actual pieces of music. It should be possible to transcribe these pieces note-for-note. The following suggestions should prove helpful:

1. Listen to the complete exercise.

2. How would you characterize the texture of the music? Are there clear melodic lines? Most piano textures and ensemble textures will have prominent melodies. Focus on these lines that you will be able to isolate.

3. All examples, even those that are contrapuntal, will have obvious harmonic implications. In more homophonic pieces, the chord structures should be quite clear and easily heard as such. Although you will not be required to supply the Roman numerals, harmonic analysis can be a great aid in hearing the music.

4. What is the structure of the music? Do you clearly hear phrase and cadence? What are the cadence types?

Finally, the CD-ROM will allow you to listen to any one exercise as many times as you wish. Early on in your work, this may be necessary. You should always try, however, to transcribe the music with as few hearings as possible. In most cases, four repetitions should be more than enough. As your skills develop, the number of hearings should decrease. You may elect at any time to see the solution to any of the exercises except for the quizzes. After comparing your solution with that on the screen, you may wish to listen one more time, concentrating on those places where you made mistakes.

The accompanying workbook provides you with staff paper already formatted with the correct number of measures for each example, along with the key and time signatures and any given pitches. You may find it useful to use scratch paper for your preliminary sketches, using the workbook only to enter your final version. Perforated Workbook pages make it easy for any of the exercises to be handed in for evaluation by your instructor.

Getting Started

The software application is complete on one CD-ROM for both Windows-compatible and Macintosh computers. The application runs directly from the CD-ROM with no installation required.

System Requirements for Windows®

- Pentium processor and Windows 95 or later. Supported systems include Windows 95 / 98 / 2000 / XP.
- 16-bit PCM sound card or General MIDI-compatible synthesizer
- CD-ROM drive

System Requirements for Macintosh™

- PowerPC™ processor with Mac OS 7.5 or later. Fully supports Macintosh OS X.
- QuickTime system extension or General MIDI-compatible synthesizer
- CD-ROM drive

Starting the Application

To run the application, simply insert the CD-ROM into your computer. The application may start automatically (Windows only). Otherwise, double-click on the "**MusicET**" startup icon appropriate for your operating system:

  MusicET   Windows operating systems

MusicET Classic Mac OS   Macintosh OS 7.5 – 9.x

  MusicET Mac OSX   Macintosh OS X

The "Autoplay" function can be set on Windows machines to automatically start a CD-ROM when inserted into the CD-ROM drive. Consult your system documentation for information.

Application File Names and Formats

The full pathname of the application for WINDOWS (assuming a CD-ROM drive "**D**") is **D:\MusicET.exe**. Double-clicking on the icon for the CD-ROM drive in the "My Computer" folder will also start the application.

For MACINTOSH, two application formats are provided on the CD. One is for older "Classic" operating systems and the other is for Macintosh OS X. Be sure to click on the startup icon appropriate for your operating system.

Monitor Settings for Windows Systems

The standard monitor resolution of 800 x 600 pixels is recommended. The font size setting for "Small fonts" (100%) is also recommended. Other resolution or font size settings may cause elements to display improperly. These items are set in the "Display" Control Panel settings.

Important:

The application is designed to run directly from the CD. *Do not copy files to your hard drive.* Doing so could create conflicts that may cause the application to fail.

Handle the CD with care. If it becomes dirty or damaged, software performance may be compromised. If necessary, the CD can be cleaned carefully with a soft cloth.

Here are some selections from the *Music for Ear Training* Help function. For more, click on the "**Help**" button in the application.

Main Menu

The first screen in the application is the Main Menu. Scroll down the window to find the desired Unit. Click on any line to select a group of exercises.

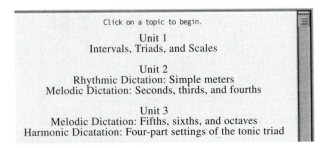

Click on a topic to begin.

Unit 1
Intervals, Triads, and Scales

Unit 2
Rhythmic Dictation: Simple meters
Melodic Dictation: Seconds, thirds, and fourths

Unit 3
Melodic Dictation: Fifths, sixths, and octaves
Harmonic Dicatation: Four-part settings of the tonic triad

 Quit the program.

 Select internal sounds or an external synthesizer. (Defaults to internal sounds.)

Choosing an example

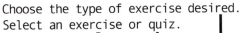
Choose the type of exercise desired. Select an exercise or quiz.

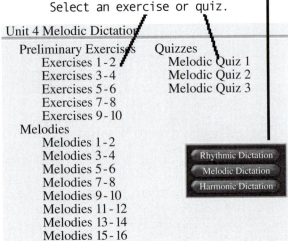

Unit 4 Melodic Dictation

Preliminary Exercises	Quizzes
Exercises 1-2	Melodic Quiz 1
Exercises 3-4	Melodic Quiz 2
Exercises 5-6	Melodic Quiz 3
Exercises 7-8	
Exercises 9-10	
Melodies	
Melodies 1-2	
Melodies 3-4	
Melodies 5-6	Rhythmic Dictation
Melodies 7-8	Melodic Dictation
Melodies 9-10	Harmonic Dictation
Melodies 11-12	
Melodies 13-14	
Melodies 15-16	

Rhythm Exercises

What to do: Listen to the example and notate it in your workbook. After making your best effort, click the "**Show Answer**" button to check your work. (Since Quizzes are intended to be graded by the instructor, answers for quizzes are not available.)

Hint: Try selecting a pitched sound, such as "harp," to better hear the durations of notes.

When you have finished an exercise, click the "**Next Example**" button to continue.

Sound controls:

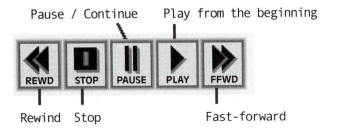

Pause / Continue   Play from the beginning

REWD   STOP   PAUSE   PLAY   FFWD

Rewind   Stop   Fast-forward

Melody Exercises

What to do: Listen to the example and notate it in your workbook. Click on "Hear tonic note" and "Hear scale" to orient yourself to the key.

After making your best effort, click the "**Show Answer**" button to check your work. Then, click the "**Next Example**" button to continue.

The "Preliminary Exercises" provide practice with basic melodic patterns.

The "Melodies" are more elaborate phrase-length tunes.

The "Quizzes" test your mastery of the material. (Since Quizzes are intended to be graded by your instructor, answers for quizzes are not available.)

Harmonic Exercises

What to do: Listen to the example and notate it in your workbook. Remember to include your harmonic analysis of the passage.

Hint: It is often a good idea to begin with the bass line before notating upper parts.

After making your best effort, click the "**Show Answer**" button to check your work. Then, click the "**Next Example**" button to continue.

The "Quizzes" test your mastery of the material. (Since Quizzes are intended to be graded by your instructor, answers for quizzes are not available.)

It is possible to choose to hear individual voices in the four-part texture. (For an added challenge, try not to over-use this function.)

⦿ woodwinds	☒ soprano
○ brass	☒ alto
○ strings	☒ tenor
○ piano	☒ bass

Keyboard Shortcuts

The keyboard commands allow you to control the application without taking your eyes off your dictation work.

SPACEBAR	Play from beginning/Stop
ENTER (Windows PC) RETURN (Mac) }	Pause play/Continue (Not enabled in Unit 1)
UP arrow key	Show the answer
RIGHT arrow key	Go on to next exercise
LEFT arrow key	Go back to previous unit

Selecting sounds and tempo

Select your preferred "General MIDI" instrumental sound from the options provided.

You can also change the tempo of an example.

tempo 100%
faster ▲
a tempo ■
slower ▼

Optimizing Computer Performance

If computer performance becomes slow or erratic, try to maximize the computer memory available. Shut down any other applications which may be open. If your computer monitor is set to a high resolution of color, you can increase performance speed by setting it back to 8-bit color, also called "256 colors." (The Music for Dictation CD-ROM does use some 16-bit images, but an 8-bit color setting will suffice.)

You can also turn off extensions in the operating system to increase available memory.

MIDI and audio

Make sure that the sound function of your computer is turned on and that the volume is turned up. A sound card is required for Windows computers. For Macintosh, the default QuickTime system extension is all that is needed.

For best sound quality, make sure that the audio output of your computer is plugged into headphones or a sound system.

If you prefer to use an external "General MIDI" synthesizer, you can route the MIDI signal to it by clicking on the "Preferences" button and selecting an alternate MIDI device. (To do this with "Classic" Macintosh systems, OMS, a freely available system utility is required.)

MUSIC
for
EAR TRAINING

Unit 1

Intervals, triads, and scales

Major and minor seconds: QUIZ NO. 1

Melodic ascending

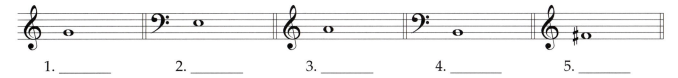

1. _____   2. _____   3. _____   4. _____   5. _____

Melodic descending

6. _____   7. _____   8. _____   9. _____   10. _____

Harmonic (lower note given)

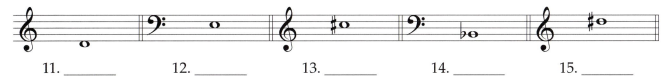

11. _____   12. _____   13. _____   14. _____   15. _____

Cumulative

(melodic, both ascending and descending, and harmonic)

16. _____   17. _____   18. _____   19. _____   20. _____

21. _____   22. _____   23. _____   24. _____   25. _____

Major and minor seconds: QUIZ NO. 2

Melodic ascending

1. _____   2. _____   3. _____   4. _____   5. _____

Melodic descending

6. _____   7. _____   8. _____   9. _____   10. _____

Harmonic (lower note given)

11. _____   12. _____   13. _____   14. _____   15. _____

Cumulative

(melodic, both ascending and descending, and harmonic)

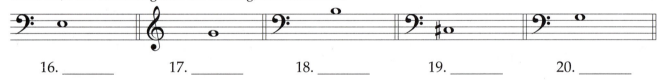

16. _____   17. _____   18. _____   19. _____   20. _____

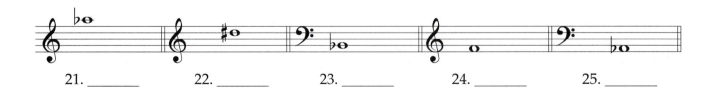

21. _____   22. _____   23. _____   24. _____   25. _____

Major and minor thirds: QUIZ NO. 1

Thirds only

Melodic ascending

1. _____   2. _____   3. _____   4. _____   5. _____

Melodic descending

6. _____   7. _____   8. _____   9. _____   10. _____

Harmonic

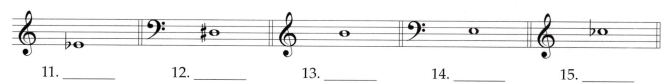

11. _____   12. _____   13. _____   14. _____   15. _____

Cumulative

16. _____   17. _____   18. _____   19. _____   20. _____

21. _____   22. _____   23. _____   24. _____   25. _____

Major and minor thirds: QUIZ NO. 2

Thirds only

Melodic ascending

1. _____   2. _____   3. _____   4. _____   5. _____

Melodic descending

6. _____   7. _____   8. _____   9. _____   10. _____

Harmonic

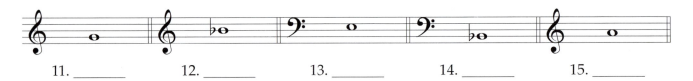

11. _____   12. _____   13. _____   14. _____   15. _____

Cumulative

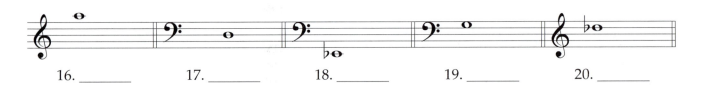

16. _____   17. _____   18. _____   19. _____   20. _____

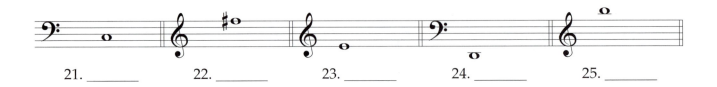

21. _____   22. _____   23. _____   24. _____   25. _____

Perfect and augmented fourths: QUIZ NO. 1

Fourths only

Melodic ascending

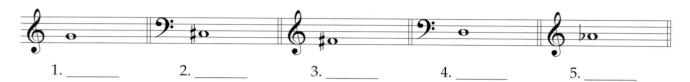

1. _____   2. _____   3. _____   4. _____   5. _____

Melodic descending

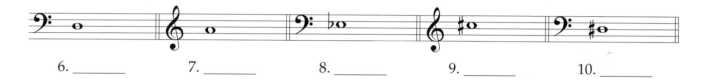

6. _____   7. _____   8. _____   9. _____   10. _____

Harmonic

11. _____   12. _____   13. _____   14. _____   15. _____

Cumulative

16. _____   17. _____   18. _____   19. _____   20. _____

21. _____   22. _____   23. _____   24. _____   25. _____

Name: _____

Perfect and augmented fourths: QUIZ NO. 2

Fourths only

Melodic ascending

1. _____   2. _____   3. _____   4. _____   5. _____

Melodic descending

6. _____   7. _____   8. _____   9. _____   10. _____

Harmonic

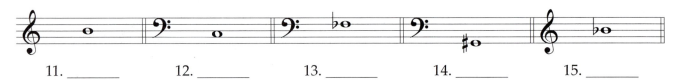

11. _____   12. _____   13. _____   14. _____   15. _____

Cumulative

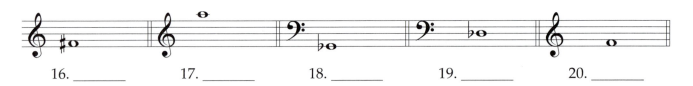

16. _____   17. _____   18. _____   19. _____   20. _____

21. _____   22. _____   23. _____   24. _____   25. _____

Perfect and diminished fifths: QUIZ NO. 1

Fifths only

Melodic ascending

1. _____   2. _____   3. _____   4. _____   5. _____

Melodic descending

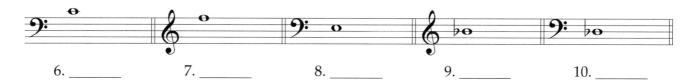

6. _____   7. _____   8. _____   9. _____   10. _____

Harmonic

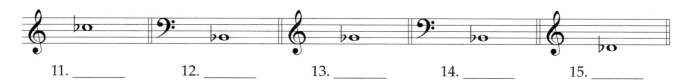

11. _____   12. _____   13. _____   14. _____   15. _____

Cumulative

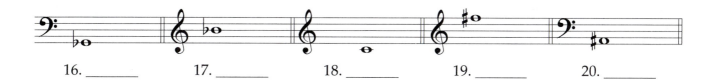

16. _____   17. _____   18. _____   19. _____   20. _____

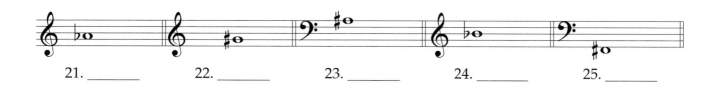

21. _____   22. _____   23. _____   24. _____   25. _____

Perfect and diminished fifths: QUIZ NO. 2

Fifths only

Melodic ascending

1. _____   2. _____   3. _____   4. _____   5. _____

Melodic descending

6. _____   7. _____   8. _____   9. _____   10. _____

Harmonic

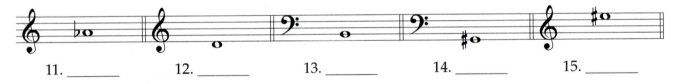

11. _____   12. _____   13. _____   14. _____   15. _____

Cumulative

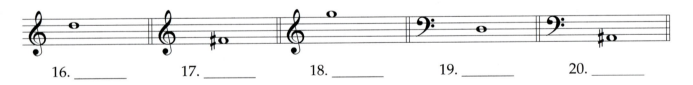

16. _____   17. _____   18. _____   19. _____   20. _____

21. _____   22. _____   23. _____   24. _____   25. _____

All perfect intervals and tritones: QUIZ NO. 1

Perfect intervals and tritones only

Melodic ascending

1. _____   2. _____   3. _____   4. _____   5. _____

Melodic descending

6. _____   7. _____   8. _____   9. _____   10. _____

Harmonic

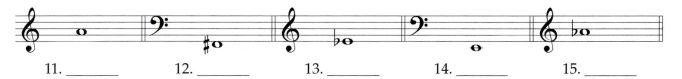

11. _____   12. _____   13. _____   14. _____   15. _____

Cumulative

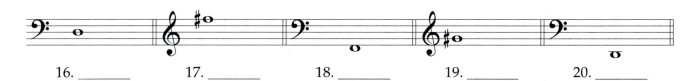

16. _____   17. _____   18. _____   19. _____   20. _____

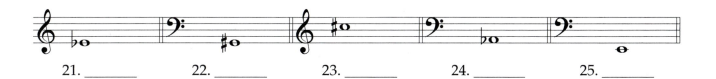

21. _____   22. _____   23. _____   24. _____   25. _____

All perfect intervals and tritones: QUIZ NO. 2

Perfect intervals and tritones only

Melodic ascending

1. _____   2. _____   3. _____   4. _____   5. _____

Melodic descending

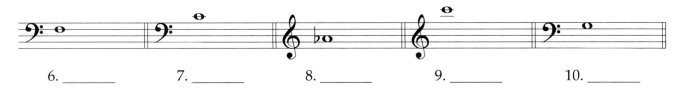

6. _____   7. _____   8. _____   9. _____   10. _____

Harmonic

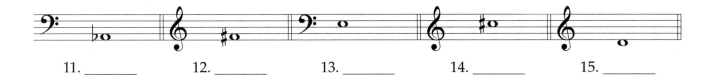

11. _____   12. _____   13. _____   14. _____   15. _____

Cumulative

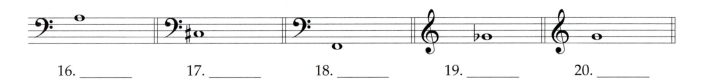

16. _____   17. _____   18. _____   19. _____   20. _____

21. _____   22. _____   23. _____   24. _____   25. _____

Major and minor sixths: QUIZ NO. 1

Sixths only

Melodic ascending

1. _____   2. _____   3. _____   4. _____   5. _____

Melodic descending

6. _____   7. _____   8. _____   9. _____   10. _____

Harmonic

11. _____   12. _____   13. _____   14. _____   15. _____

Cumulative

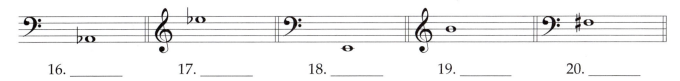

16. _____   17. _____   18. _____   19. _____   20. _____

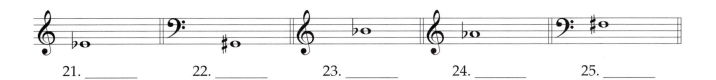

21. _____   22. _____   23. _____   24. _____   25. _____

Name: _____

Major and minor sixths: QUIZ NO. 2

Sixths only

Melodic ascending

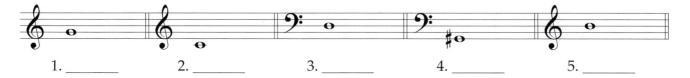

1. _____ 2. _____ 3. _____ 4. _____ 5. _____

Melodic descending

6. _____ 7. _____ 8. _____ 9. _____ 10. _____

Harmonic

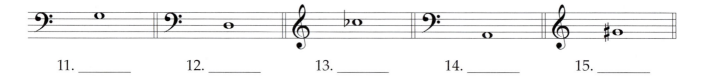

11. _____ 12. _____ 13. _____ 14. _____ 15. _____

Cumulative

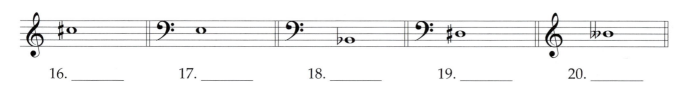

16. _____ 17. _____ 18. _____ 19. _____ 20. _____

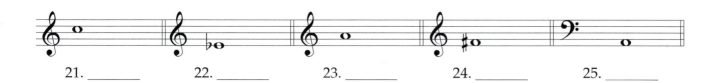

21. _____ 22. _____ 23. _____ 24. _____ 25. _____

Major and minor sevenths: QUIZ NO. 1

Sevenths only

Melodic ascending

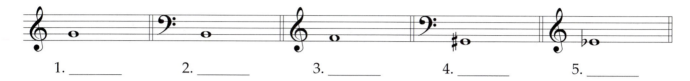

1. _____   2. _____   3. _____   4. _____   5. _____

Melodic descending

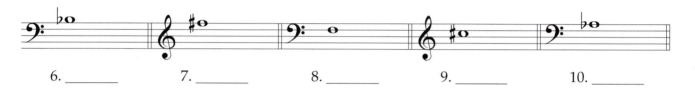

6. _____   7. _____   8. _____   9. _____   10. _____

Harmonic

11. _____   12. _____   13. _____   14. _____   15. _____

Cumulative

16. _____   17. _____   18. _____   19. _____   20. _____

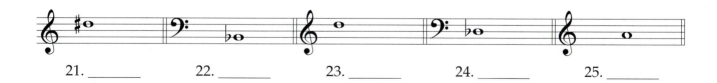

21. _____   22. _____   23. _____   24. _____   25. _____

Major and minor sevenths: QUIZ NO. 2

Sevenths only

Melodic ascending

1. _____   2. _____   3. _____   4. _____   5. _____

Melodic descending

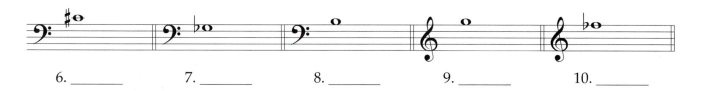

6. _____   7. _____   8. _____   9. _____   10. _____

Harmonic

11. _____   12. _____   13. _____   14. _____   15. _____

Cumulative

16. _____   17. _____   18. _____   19. _____   20. _____

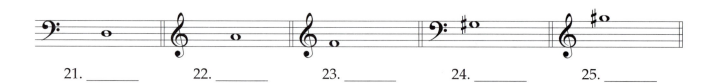

21. _____   22. _____   23. _____   24. _____   25. _____

All intervals: QUIZ NO. 1

1. _____   2. _____   3. _____   4. _____   5. _____

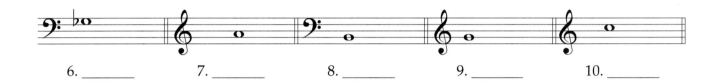

6. _____   7. _____   8. _____   9. _____   10. _____

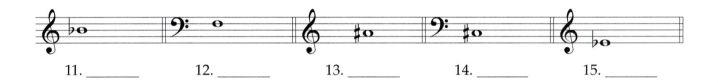

11. _____   12. _____   13. _____   14. _____   15. _____

16. _____   17. _____   18. _____   19. _____   20. _____

21. _____   22. _____   23. _____   24. _____   25. _____

All intervals: QUIZ NO. 2

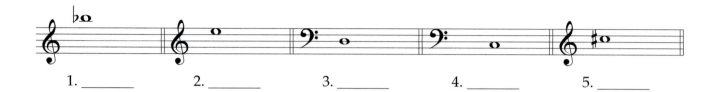

1. _____ 2. _____ 3. _____ 4. _____ 5. _____

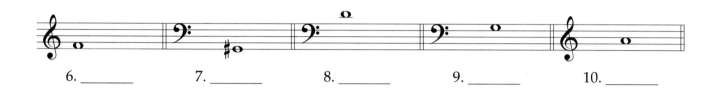

6. _____ 7. _____ 8. _____ 9. _____ 10. _____

11. _____ 12. _____ 13. _____ 14. _____ 15. _____

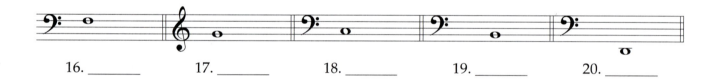

16. _____ 17. _____ 18. _____ 19. _____ 20. _____

21. _____ 22. _____ 23. _____ 24. _____ 25. _____

Major and minor triads: QUIZ NO. 1

1. _____   2. _____   3. _____   4. _____   5. _____

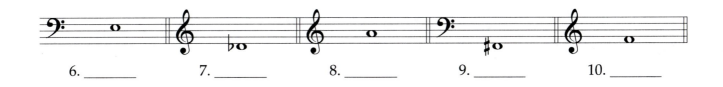

6. _____   7. _____   8. _____   9. _____   10. _____

Major and minor triads: QUIZ NO. 2

1. _____ 2. _____ 3. _____ 4. _____ 5. _____

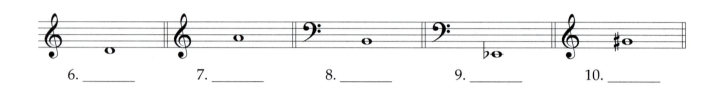

6. _____ 7. _____ 8. _____ 9. _____ 10. _____

Introducing diminished triads: QUIZ NO. 1

1. _____   2. _____   3. _____   4. _____   5. _____

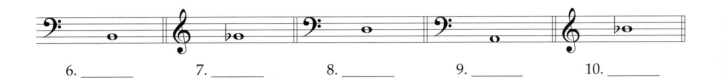

6. _____   7. _____   8. _____   9. _____   10. _____

Introducing diminished triads: QUIZ NO. 2

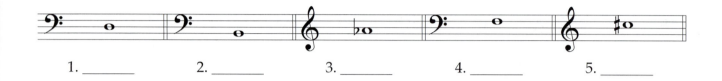

1. _____   2. _____   3. _____   4. _____   5. _____

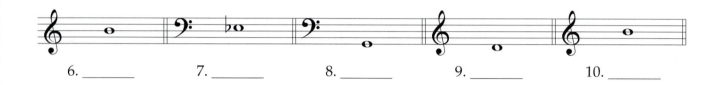

6. _____   7. _____   8. _____   9. _____   10. _____

Introducing augmented triads: QUIZ NO. 1

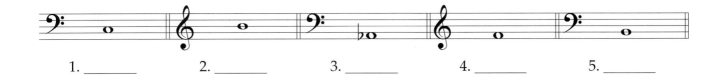

1. _____   2. _____   3. _____   4. _____   5. _____

6. _____   7. _____   8. _____   9. _____   10. _____

Name: _____

Introducing augmented triads: QUIZ NO. 2

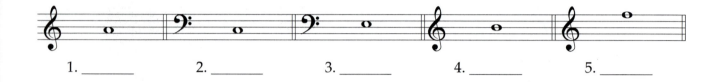

1. _____   2. _____   3. _____   4. _____   5. _____

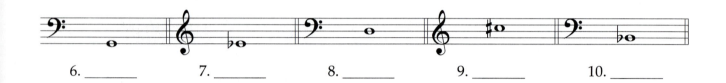

6. _____   7. _____   8. _____   9. _____   10. _____

Class: _____   Name: _____

Professor: _____

Major and minor scales: QUIZ NO. 1

1. _____

2. _____

3. _____

4. _____

5. _____

6. _____

7. _____

8. _____

9. _____

10. _____

Major and minor scales: QUIZ NO. 2

1. _____

2. _____

3. _____

4. _____

5. _____

6. _____

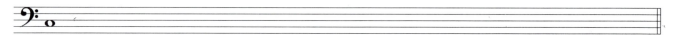

7. _____

8. _____

9. _____

10. _____

Unit 2

Rhythmic Dictation: Simple Meters

1.

2.

3.

4.

5.

6.

7.

8.

9.

10.

11.

12.

13.

14.

Name: _____

Rhythmic Dictation: QUIZ NO. 1

1.

2.

3.

4.

5.

Name: _____

Rhythmic Dictation: QUIZ NO. 2

1.

2.

3.

4.

5.

Rhythmic Dictation: QUIZ NO. 3

1.

2.

3.

4.

5.

Melodic Dictation: Seconds, thirds, and fourths

Preliminary Exercises

1.

2.

3.

4.

5.

6.

7.

8.

9.

10.

11.

12.

13.

14.

15.

16.

17.

18.

Melodies

Allegretto

1.

Serioso

2.

Briskly

3.

Moderato

4.

Lento

5.

Giocoso

6.

Deliberamente

7.

Moderato

8.

Cantabile

9.

Tempo di Valse

10.

Andante

11.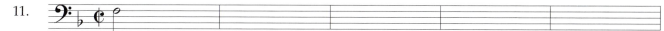

Allegro ma non troppo

12.

Waltz

13..

Cantabile

14.

Melodic Dictation: QUIZ NO. 1

Allegretto

1.

Andante

2.

Eroico

3.

Allegro

4.

Animato

5.

Melodic Dictation: QUIZ NO. 2

Lento

1.

Andante

2.

Comodo

3.

Moderato

4.

Giovale

5.

Melodic Dictation: QUIZ NO. 3

1. Giocoso

2. Waltz

3. Cantabile

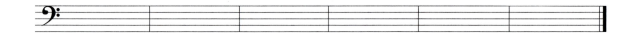

4. Stately

5. Semplice

Unit 3

Melodic Dictation: Fifths, sixths, and octaves

Preliminary Exercises

Name: _____

8.

9.

10.

11.

12.

13.

14.

15.

16.

17.

18.

Melodies

1.
Moderato

2.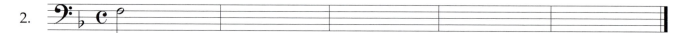
Marziale

3.
Andantino

4.
Dolce

5.
Cantabile

Moderato

6.

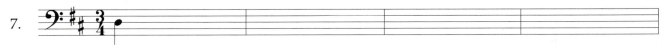

Allegro moderato

7.

Grazioso

8.

Allegretto

9.

Largamente

10.

11. Con moto
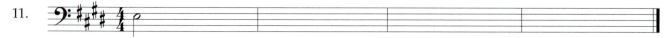

12. Cantabile

13. Andante
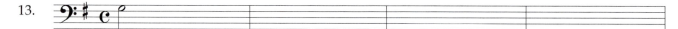

14. Lento ma non troppo

Melodic Dictation: QUIZ NO. 1

Allegretto

1.

Allegro

2.

Lento

3.

Moderato

4.

Largamente

5.

Melodic Dictation: QUIZ NO. 2

1.
Cantabile

2.
Moderato

3.
Vivo

4.
Tranquillo

Spiritoso

5.

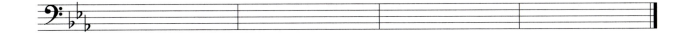

Melodic Dictation: QUIZ NO. 3

Andante

1.

Moderato assai

2.

Allegro ma non troppo

3.

Cantabile

4.

Moderato

5.

Harmonic Dictation: Four part settings of the tonic triad

1.
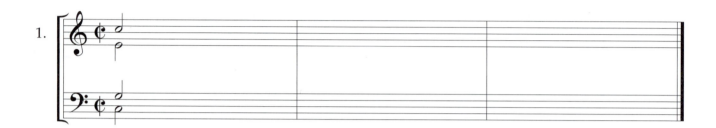

2.
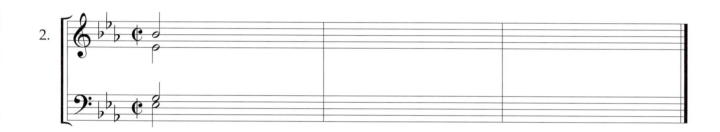

3.
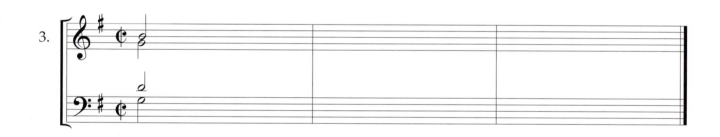

4.

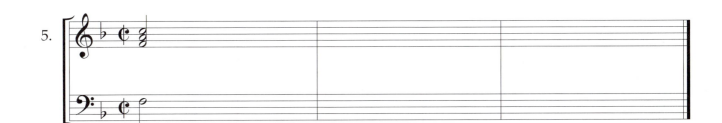

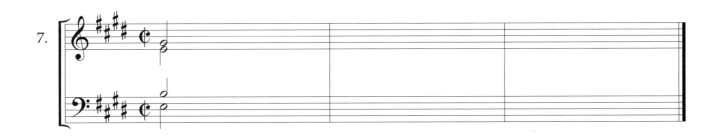

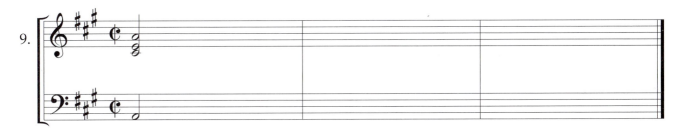

Harmonic Dictation: QUIZ NO. 1

1.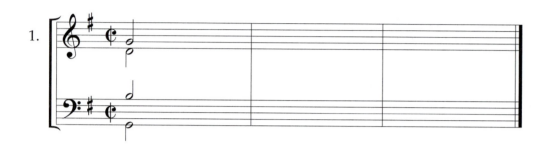

2.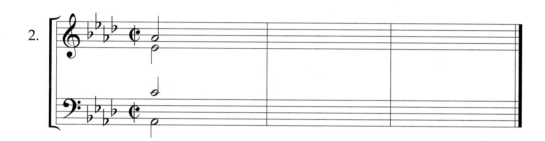

3.

Harmonic Dictation: QUIZ NO. 2

1.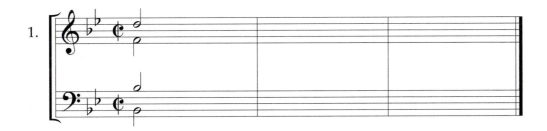

2.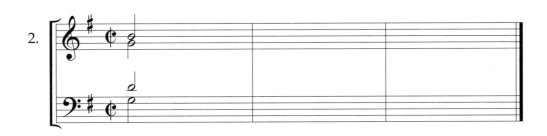

3.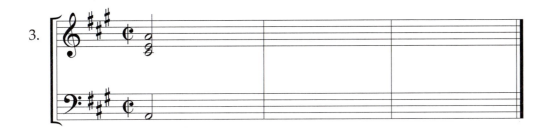

Harmonic Dictation: QUIZ NO. 3

1.
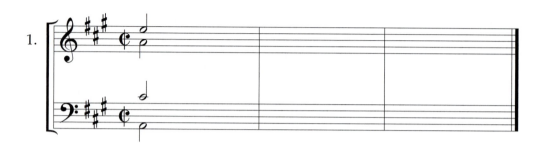

2.
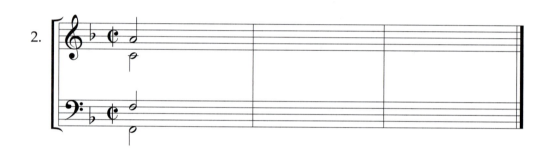

3.
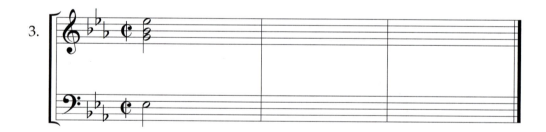

Unit 4

Rhythmic Dictation: Beat subdivision by 2

1. $\frac{2}{4}$

2. $\frac{3}{4}$

3. $\mathbf{C}$

4. $\frac{3}{8}$

5. $\mathbf{\phi}$

6. $\frac{3}{4}$

7. $\mathbf{C}$

8.

9.

10.

11.

12.

13. $\frac{3}{2}$

14. $\frac{4}{8}$

15. $\frac{3}{8}$

16. $\mathbf{C}$

Name: _____

Rhythmic Dictation: QUIZ NO. 1

1.

2.

3.

4.

5.

Rhythmic Dictation: QUIZ NO. 2

1.

2.

3.

4.

5.

Rhythmic Dictation: QUIZ NO. 3

1.

2.

3.

4.

5.

Melodic Dictation: The tonic triad and dominant seventh

Preliminary Exercises

1.

2.

3.

4.

5.

6.

7.

8.

9.

10.

Melodies

1. Allegretto

2. Poco animato

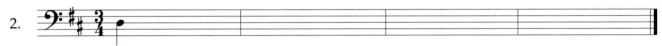

3. Allegro

4. Semplice

5.

Moderato

6.

Cantabile

7.

Moderato

8.

Maestoso

9.

Grazioso

10. Andante cantabile

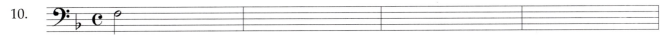

11. Giocoso

12. Minuet

13. Marziale

14. **Andante**

15. **Cantabile**

16. **Allegro assai**

Melodic Dictation: QUIZ NO. 1

Adagietto

1.

Ländler

2.

Cantabile

3.

4.

Giocoso

5.

Allegro ma non troppo

Melodic Dictation: QUIZ NO. 2

Con moto

1.

Allegretto

2.

Moderato

3.

Allegro

4.

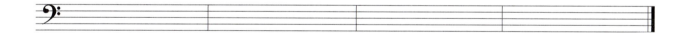

Andantino

5.

Melodic Dictation: QUIZ NO. 3

Minuet

1.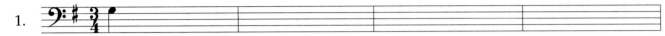

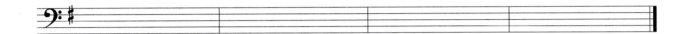

Moderato

2.

Con brio

3.

Cantabile

4.

Espressivo

5.

Harmonic Dictation: The tonic triad and dominant seventh

Basic Progressions

1.

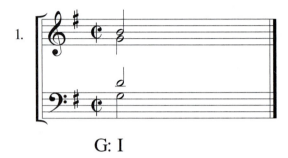

G: I

2.

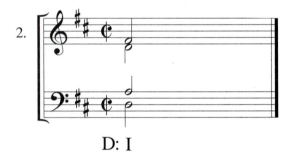

D: I

3.

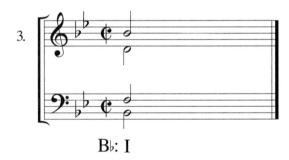

B♭: I

4.

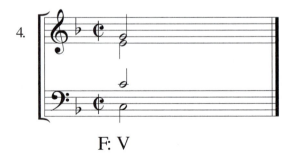

F: V

5.

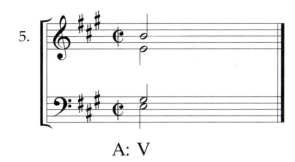

A: V

6.

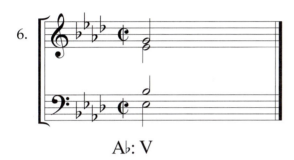

A♭: V

7.

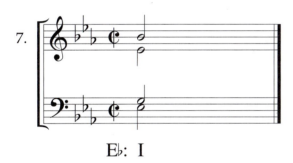

E♭: I

8.

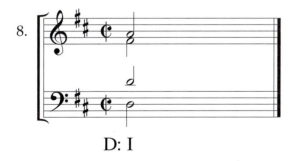

D: I

9.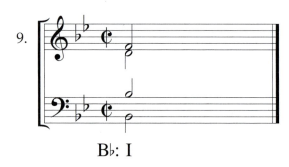

        B♭: I

10.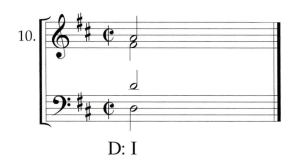

        D: I

11.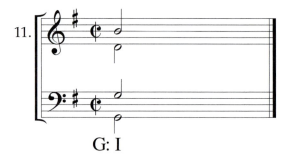

        G: I

12.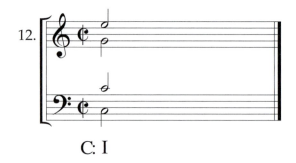

        C: I

13.

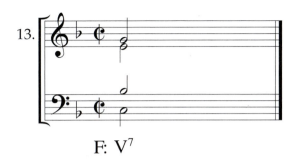

F: V^7

14.

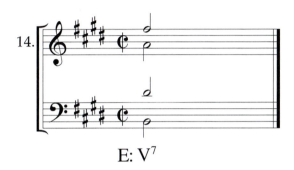

E: V^7

15.

E♭: V^7

16.

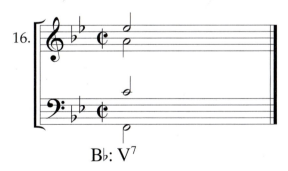

B♭: V^7

17.

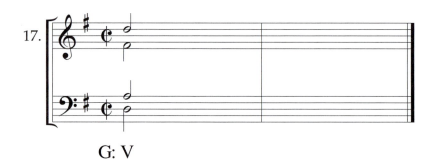

G: V

18.

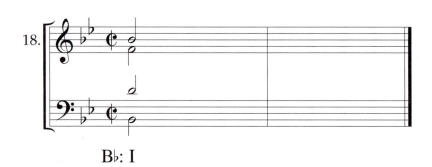

B♭: I

19.

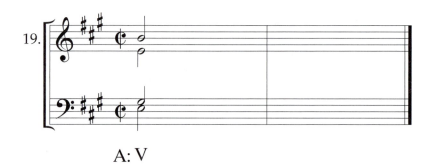

A: V

20.

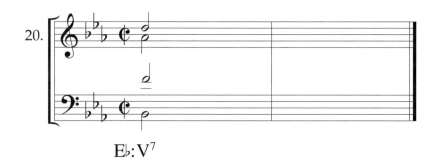

E♭: V⁷

21.

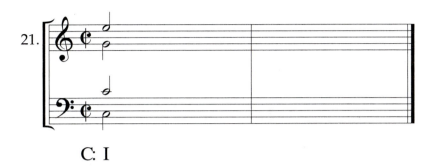

C: I

22.

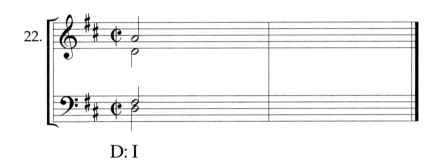

D: I

23.

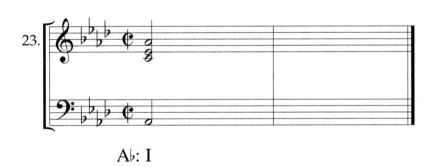

A♭: I

24.

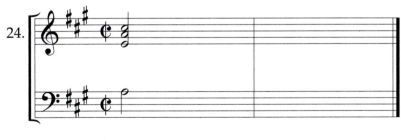

A: I

25.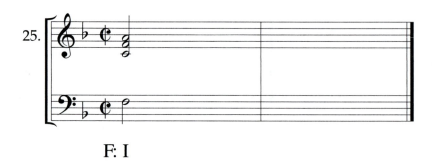

F: I

26.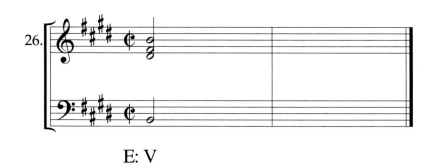

E: V

27.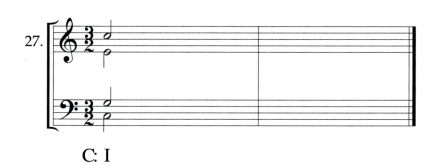

C: I

28.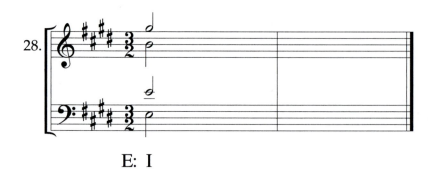

E: I

29.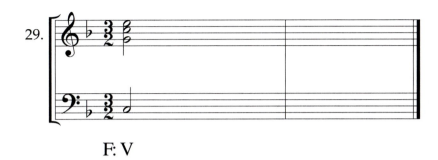

F: V

30.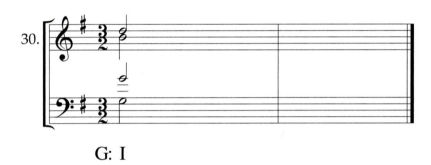

G: I

31.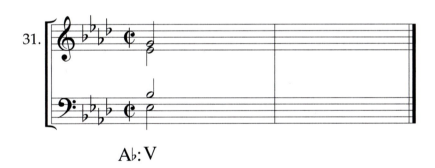

A♭: V

32.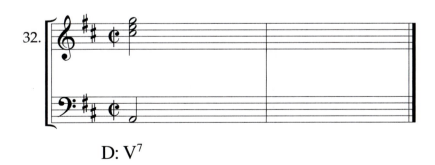

D: V^7

33.
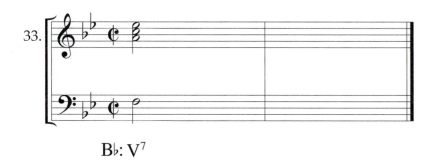

Bb: V^7

34.
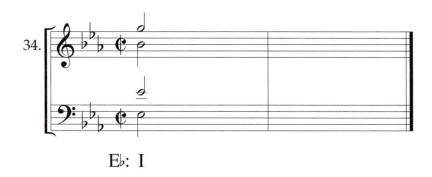

Eb: I

35.
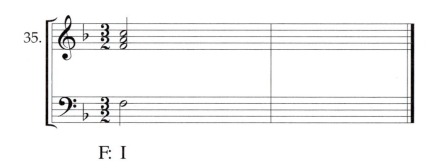

F: I

36.
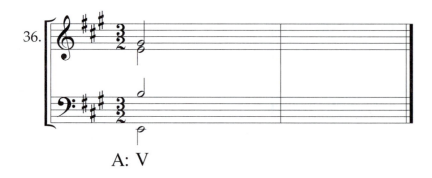

A: V

Phrase-length Exercises

1.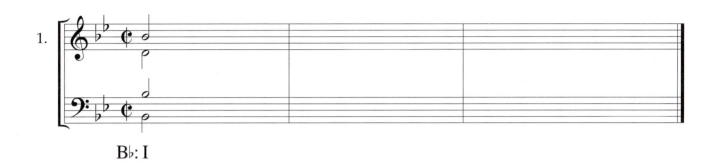

   B♭: I

2.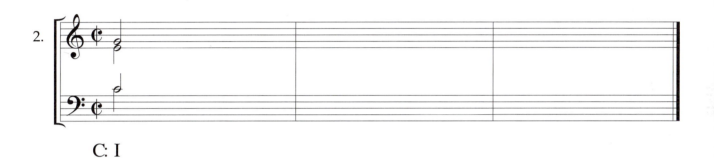

   C: I

3.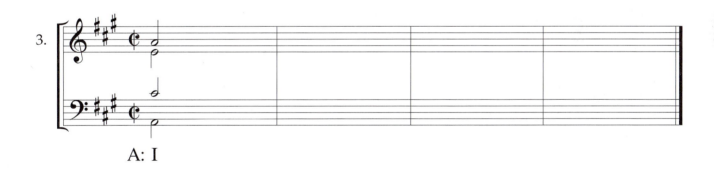

   A: I

4.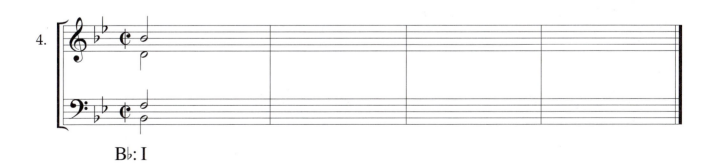

   B♭: I

5.

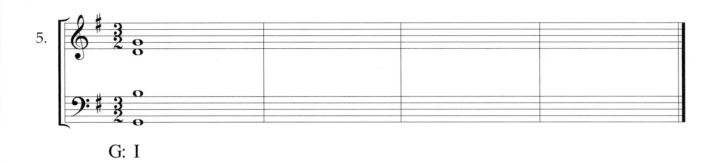

G: I

6.

F: I

7.

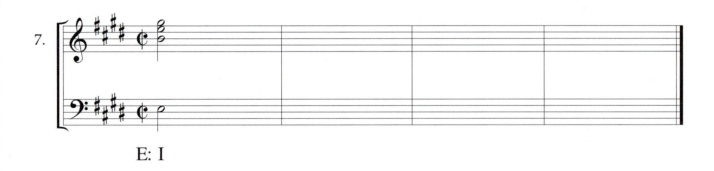

E: I

8.

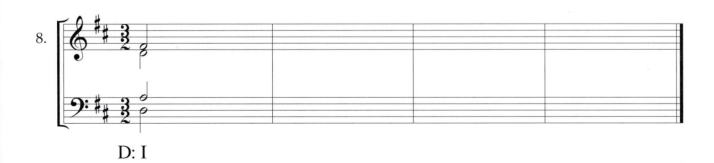

D: I

9.

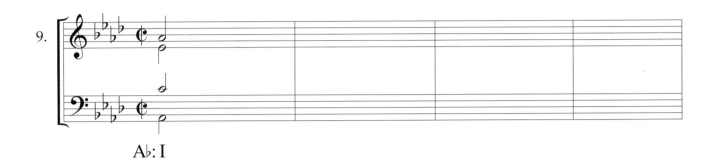

Ab: I

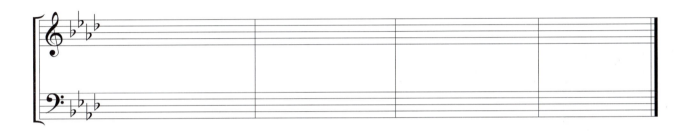

10.

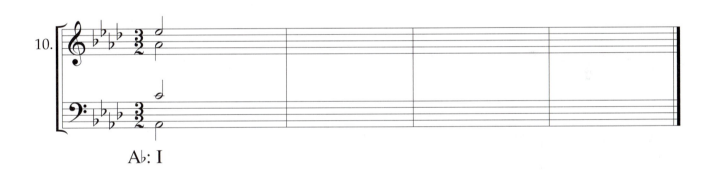

Ab: I

Harmonic Dictation: QUIZ NO. 1

1.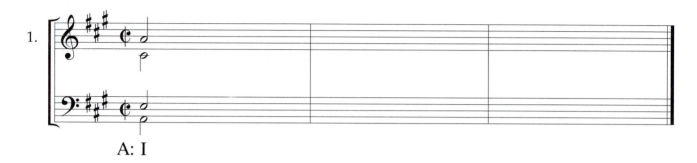

A: I

2.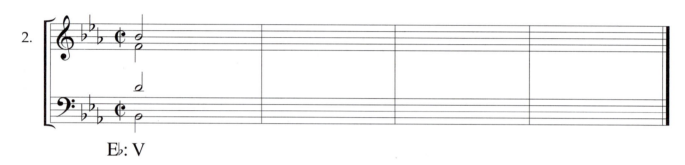

E♭: V

3.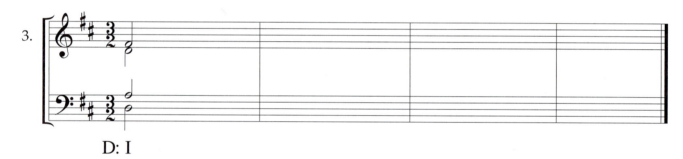

D: I

4.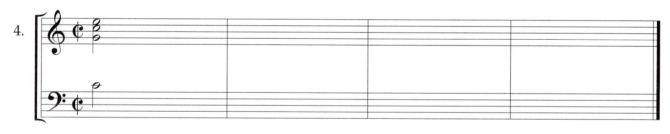

C: I

5.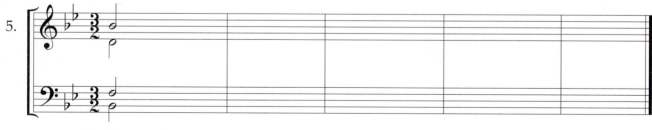

B♭: I

Harmonic Dictation: QUIZ NO. 2

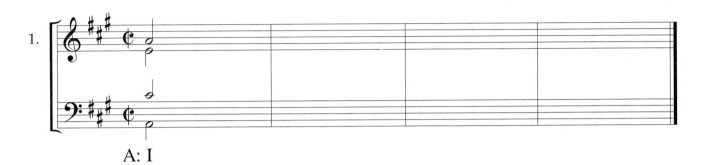

1.

A: I

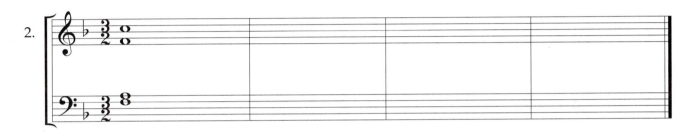

2.

F: I

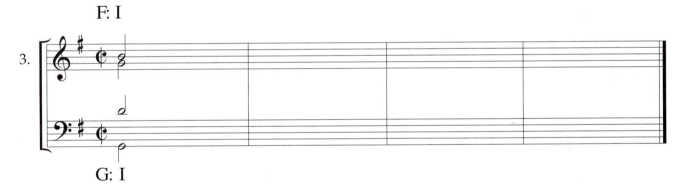

3.

G: I

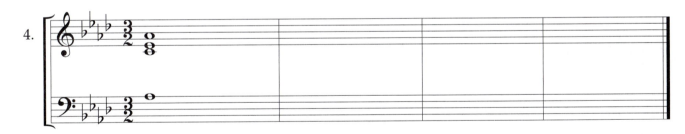

4.

A♭: I

5.

E: I

Harmonic Dictation: QUIZ NO. 3

1.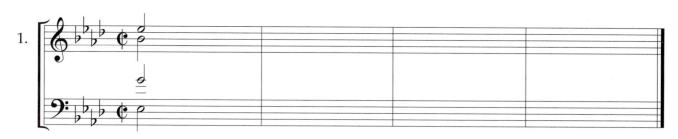

      Ab: V

2.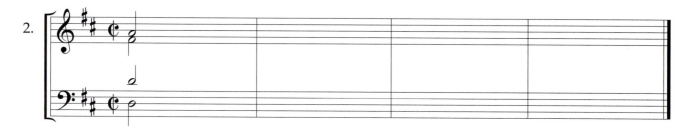

      D: I

3.

      A: I

4.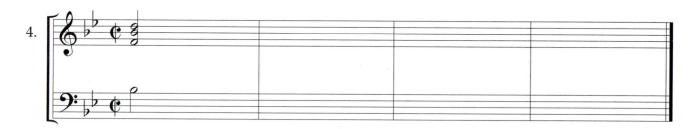

      Bb: I

5.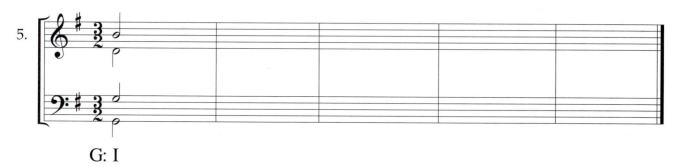

      G: I

Unit 5

Rhythmic Dictation: Beat subdivision by 4, Anacrusis

1.

2.

3.

4.

5.

6.

7.

8.

9.

10.

11.

12.

13.

14.

15.

16.

Class:

Professor:

Name: _____

Rhythmic Dictation: QUIZ NO. 1

1.

2.

3.

4.

5.

Rhythmic Dictation: QUIZ NO. 3

1.

2.

3.

4.

5.

Melodic Dictation: Primary triads and the dominant seventh

Preliminary Exercises

1.

2.

3.

4.

5.

6.

Melodies

1. Not too fast

2. Cantabile

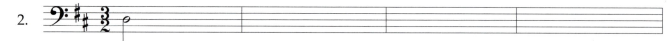

3. Moderato

4. Andante

Allegro

5.

Giocoso

6.

Andantino

7.

Allegretto

8.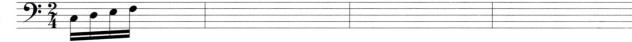

Moderato

9.

Allegro

10.

Tempo giusto

11.

Animato

12.

Larghetto

13.

14. Allegretto

15. Leggiero

16. March

Melodic Dictation: QUIZ NO. 1

Allegro ma non troppo

1.

Ländler

2.

Marziale

3.

Moderato

4.

Andantino

5.

Melodic Dictation: QUIZ NO. 2

Grazioso

1.

Moderato

2.

Allegro moderato

3.

Allegro

4.

Allegretto

5.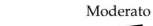

Melodic Dictation: QUIZ NO. 3

Semplice

1.

Cantabile

2.

Allegro

3.

4.

Spiritoso

5.

Dolce

Harmonic Dictation: Primary triads and the dominant seventh; Cadential tonic six-four

Basic Progressions

Primary triads and the dominant seventh

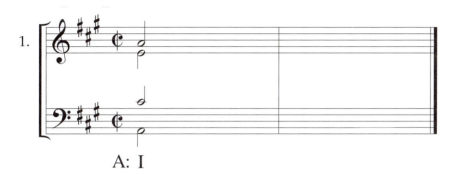

1.

A: I

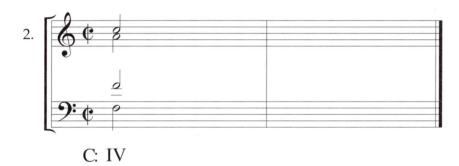

2.

C: IV

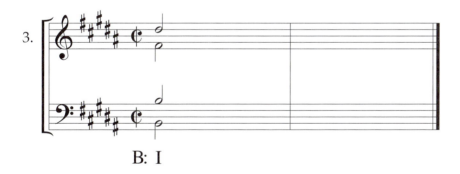

3.

B: I

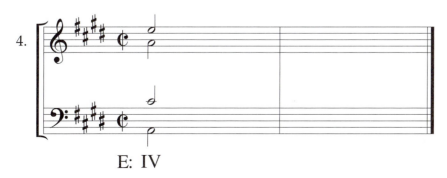

4.

E: IV

5.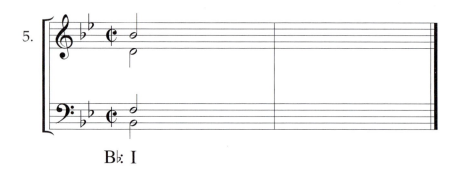

B♭: I

6.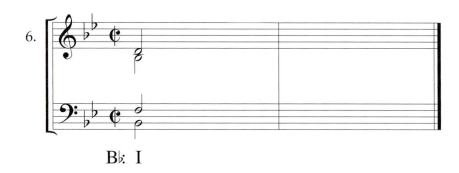

B♭: I

7.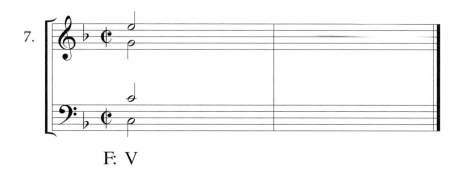

F: V

8.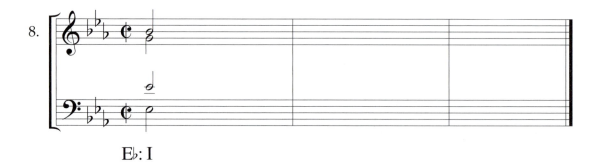

E♭: I

Class: _____ Name: _____

Professor: _____

9.

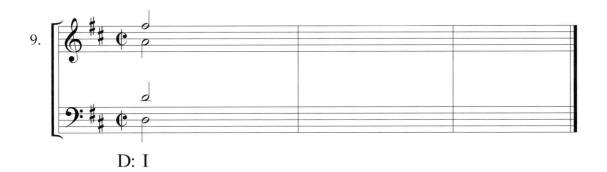

D: I

10.

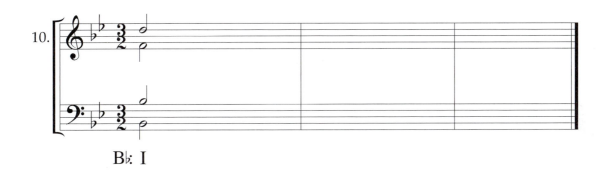

B♭: I

Cadential tonic six-four

11.

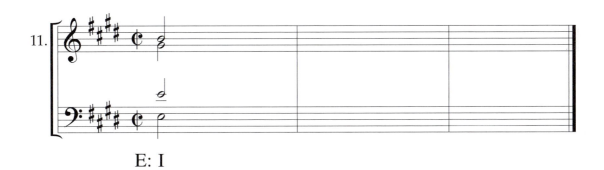

E: I

12.

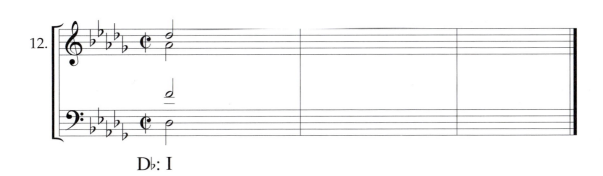

D♭: I

13.

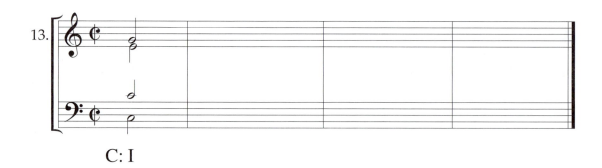

C: I

14.

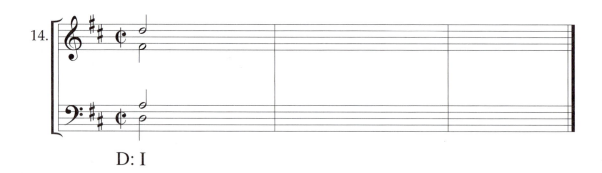

D: I

15.

A♭: I

16.

G: I

Phrase-length Exercises

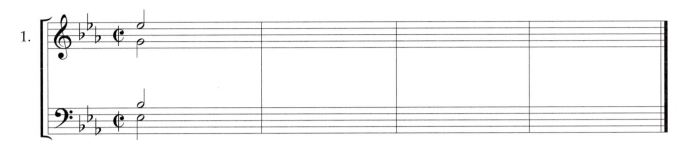

E♭: I

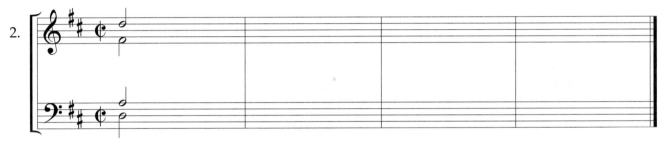

D: I

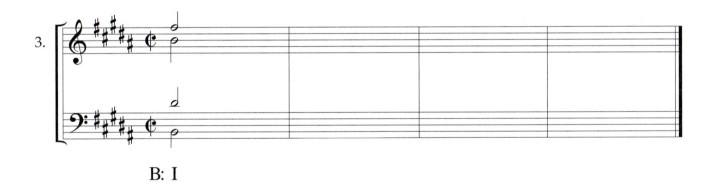

B: I

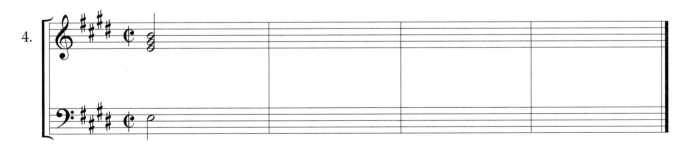

E: I

5.

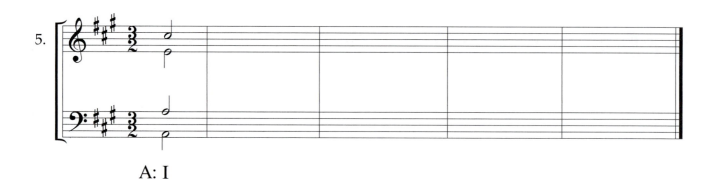

A: I

6.

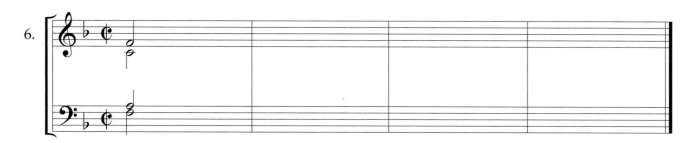

F: I

7.

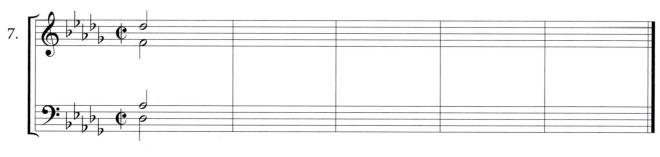

D♭: I

8.

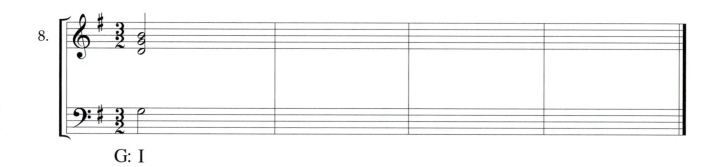

G: I

9.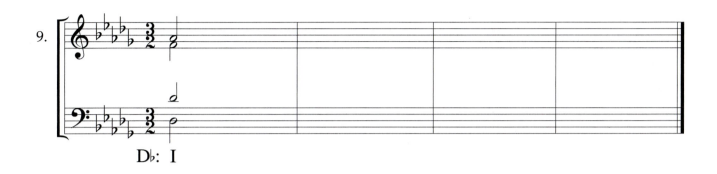

Db: I

10.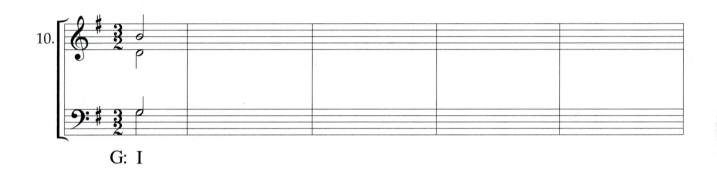

G: I

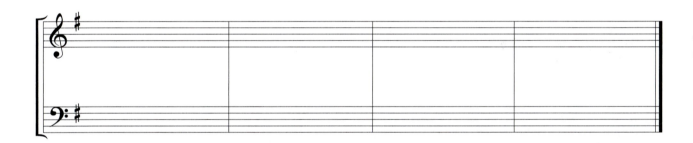

Harmonic Dictation: QUIZ NO. 1

1.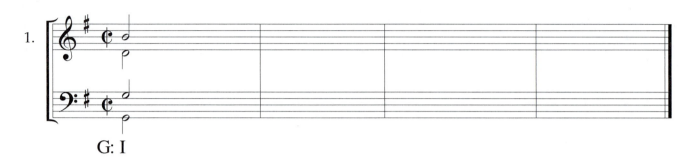

G: I

2.

Bb: I

3.

C: I

4.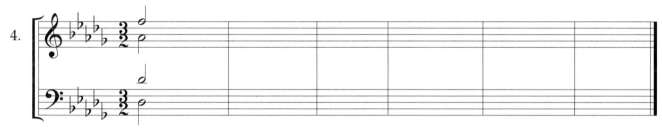

Db: I

5.

Eb: I

Harmonic Dictation: QUIZ NO. 2

1.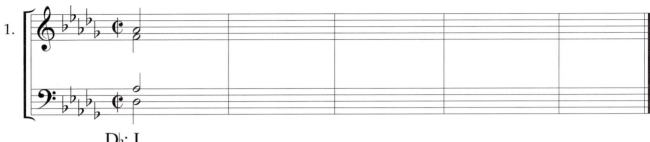

Db: I

2.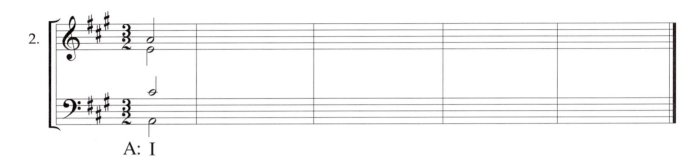

A: I

3.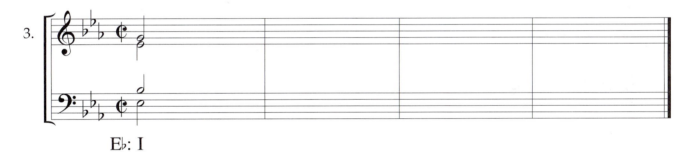

Eb: I

4.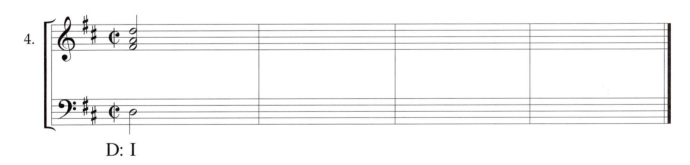

D: I

5.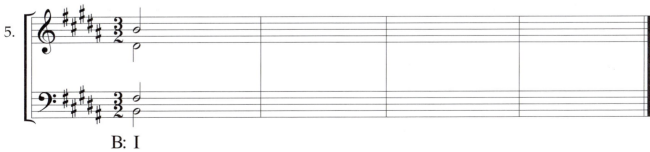

B: I

Harmonic Dictation: QUIZ NO. 3

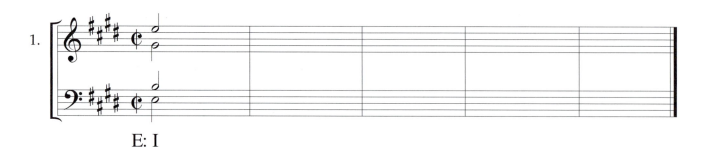

1.

E: I

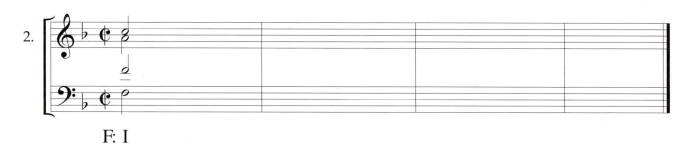

2.

F: I

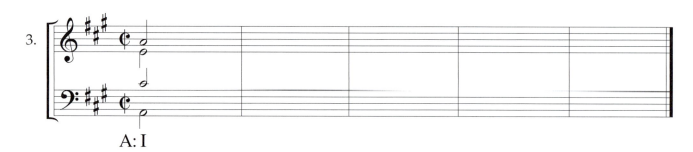

3.

A: I

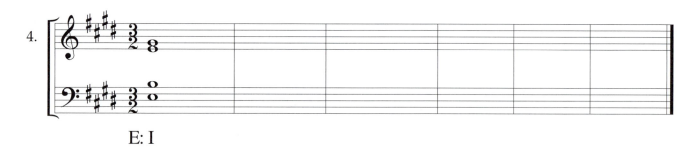

4.

E: I

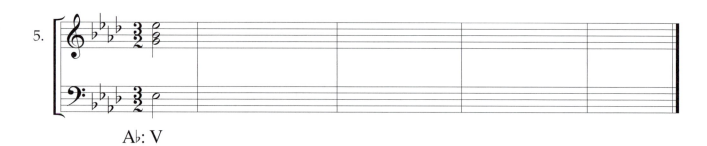

5.

A♭: V

Unit 6

Rhythmic Dictation: Dots and ties

1.

2.

3.

4.

5.

6.

7.

8.

9.

10.

11.

12.

13.

14.

15.

16.

Rhythmic Dictation: QUIZ NO. 1

1. $\quad$ 𝄆 $\frac{2}{4}$

2. $\quad$ 𝄆 $\frac{3}{2}$

3. $\quad$ 𝄆 $\frac{4}{4}$

4. $\quad$ 𝄆 $\frac{3}{4}$

5. $\quad$ 𝄆 ¢

Rhythmic Dictation: QUIZ NO. 2

1.

2.

3.

4.

5.

Rhythmic Dictation: QUIZ NO. 3

1.

2.

3.

4.

5.

Melodic Dictation: Minor mode

Preliminary Exercises

1.

2.

3.

4.

5.

6.

Melodies

Grazioso

1.

Andantino

2.

Con forza

3.

Moderato

4.

Allegretto

5.

Moderato

6.

Vigoroso

7.

Energico

8.

Cantabile

9.

Dolce

10.

Adagietto

11.

Deciso

12.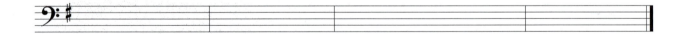

Comodo

13.

Allegro

14.

Espressivo

15.

Con moto

16.

Melodic Dictation: QUIZ NO. 1

Buffo

1.
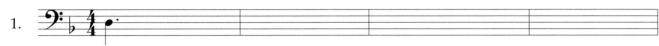

Adagietto

2.

Con moto

3.

Ben marcato

4.

5. Valse

Melodic Dictation: QUIZ NO. 2

Moderato

1.

Allegro

2.

Andante

3.

Grazioso

4.

Solenne

5.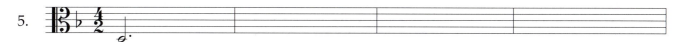

Melodic Dictation: QUIZ NO. 3

Andante

1.

Con forza

2.

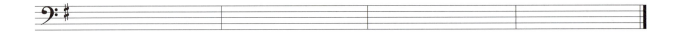

Grazioso

3.

Doloroso

4.

5. **Geschwind**

Harmonic Dictation: Minor mode; First inversion of triads

Basic Progressions

Minor mode

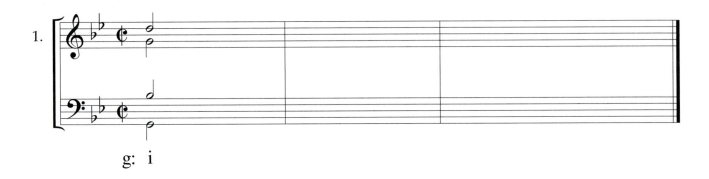

1.

g: i

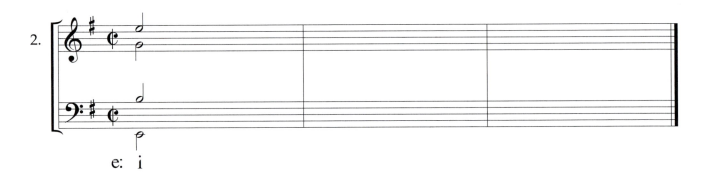

2.

e: i

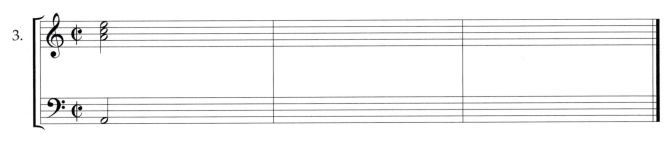

3.

a: i

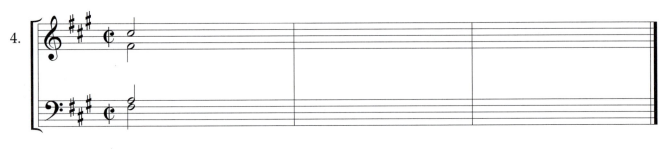

4.

f♯: i

5.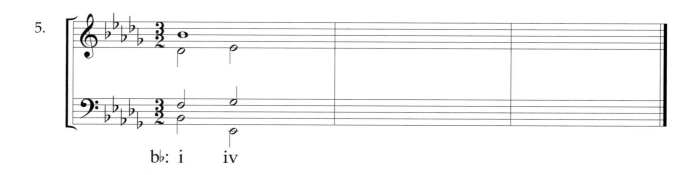

b♭: i   iv

6.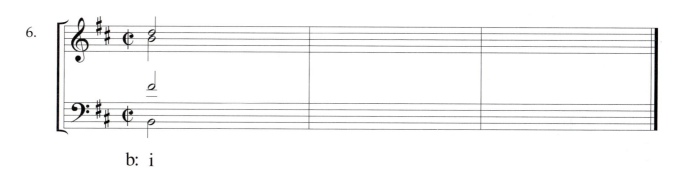

b: i

First inversion of triads

7.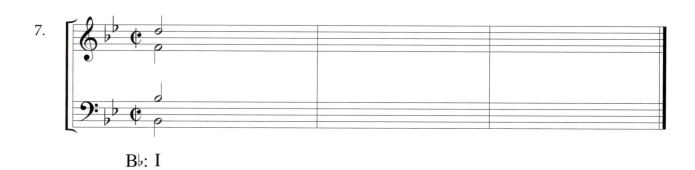

B♭: I

8.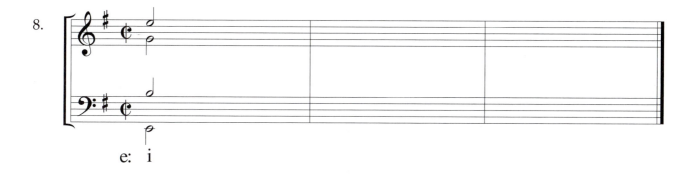

e: i

9.

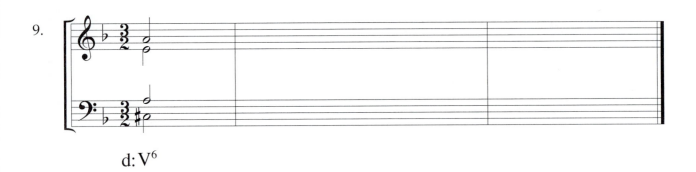

d: V⁶

10.

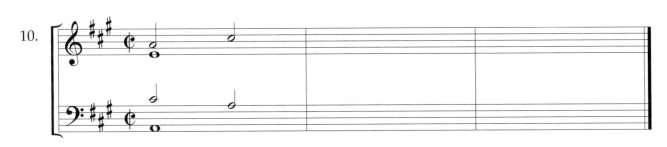

A: I

11.

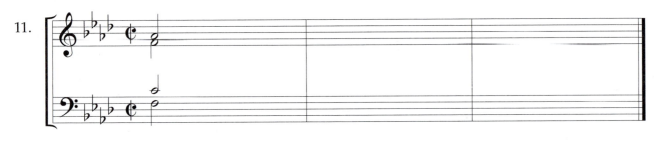

f: i

12.

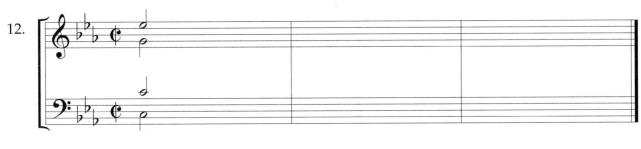

c: i

13.

B♭: I

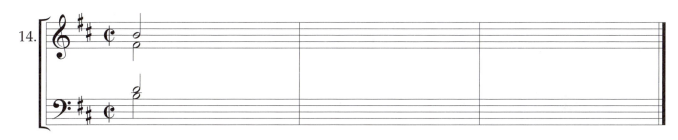

14.

b: i

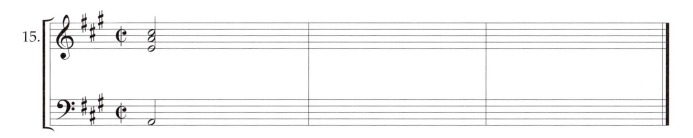

15.

A: I

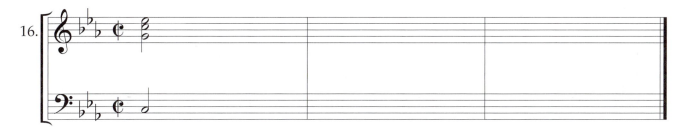

16.

c: i

Phrase-length Exercises

1.
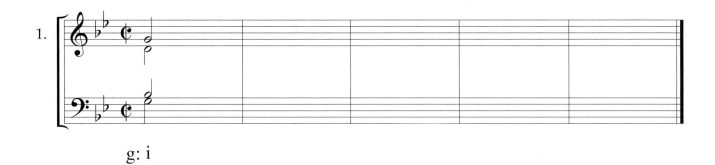

    g: i

2.
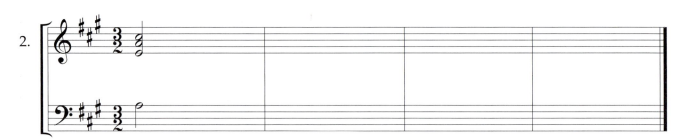

    A: I

3.
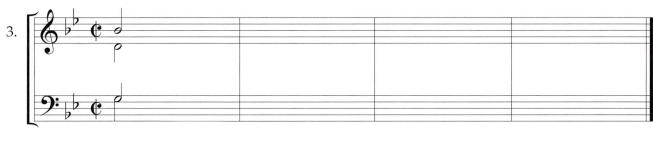

    g: i

4.
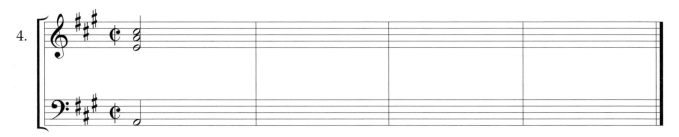

    A: I

5.

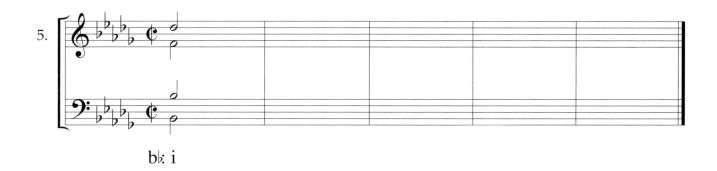

b♭: i

6.

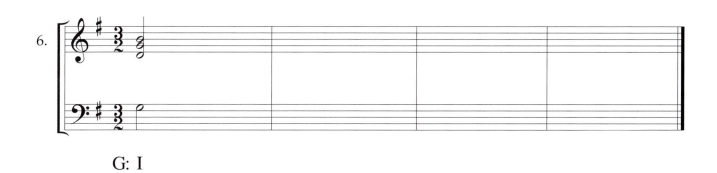

G: I

7.

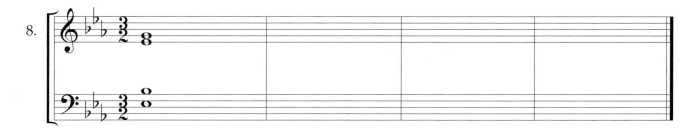

b: i

8.

E♭: I

9.

e: i

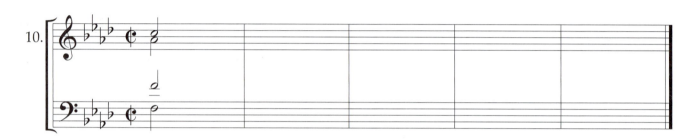

10.

f: i

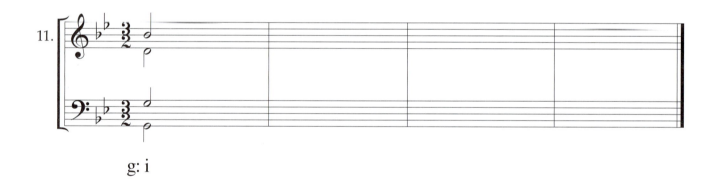

11.

g: i

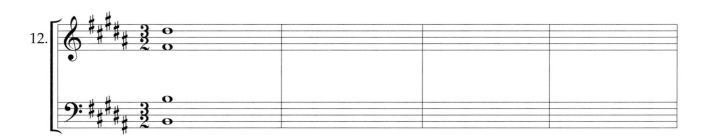

12.

B: I

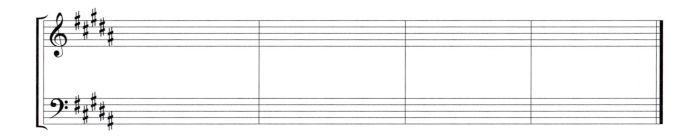

Harmonic Dictation: QUIZ NO. 1

1.

F: I

2.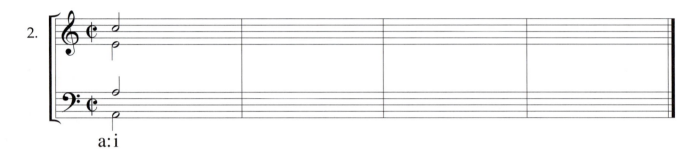

a: i

3.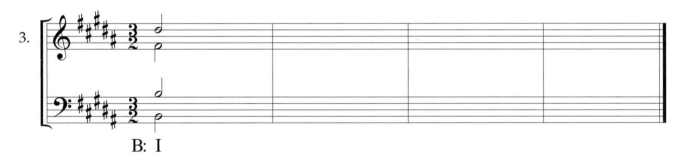

B: I

4.

c: i

5.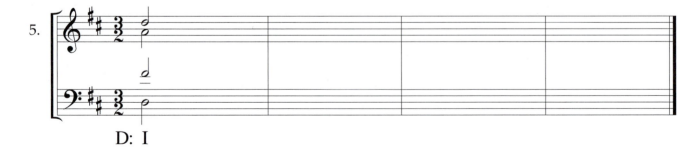

D: I

Harmonic Dictation: QUIZ NO. 2

1.
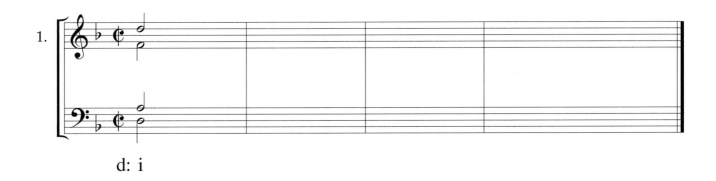

       d: i

2.
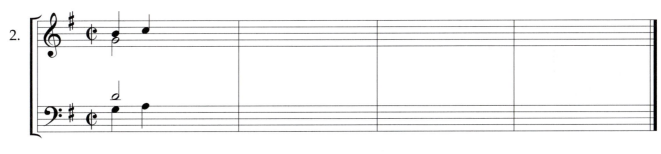

       G: I ___

3.
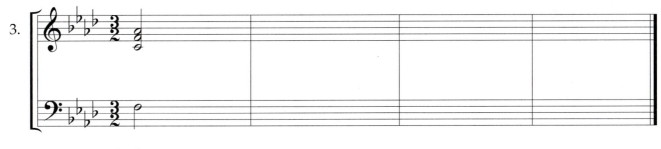

       f: i

4.
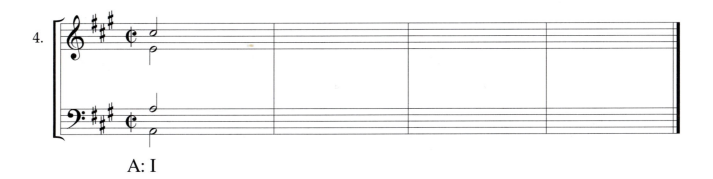

       A: I

5.

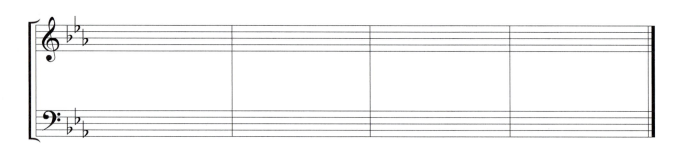

c: i

Harmonic Dictation: QUIZ NO. 3

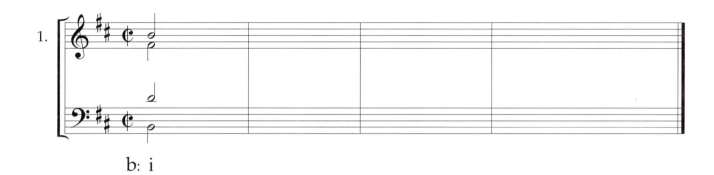

1.

b: i

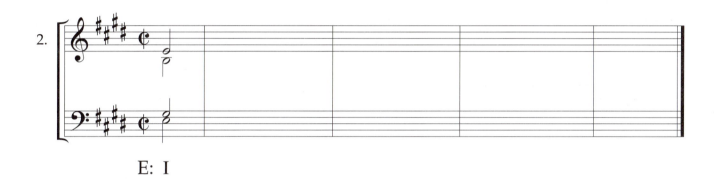

2.

E: I

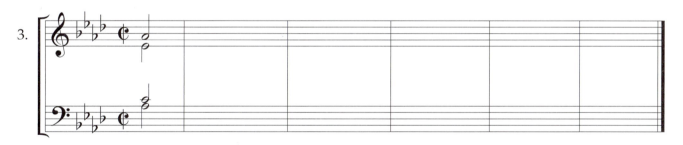

3.

A♭: I

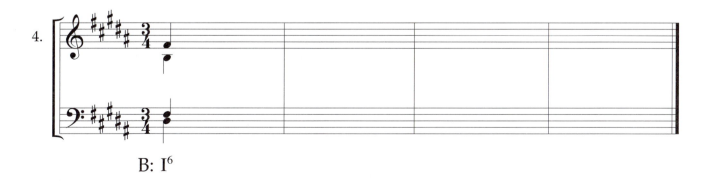

4.

B: I⁶

5.

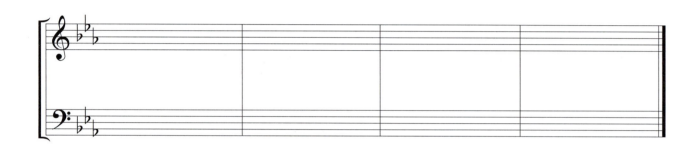

c: i

Unit 7 ═══════════════════

Melodic Dictation: The supertonic triad

Preliminary Exercises

1.

2.

3.

4.

5.

6.

Melodies

Cantabile

1.

Andante

2.

Valse triste

3.

Tempo di Polka

4.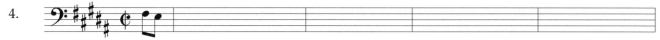

5. Leggiero

6. Lively

7. Giocoso

8. Lento

Allegro moderato

9.

Amoroso

10.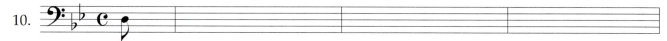

Spiritoso

11.

Grave

12.

13.
Zart

14.
Allegretto

Melodic Dictation: QUIZ NO. 1

1. Andantino

2. Allegro spiritoso

3. Allegro

4. Andante

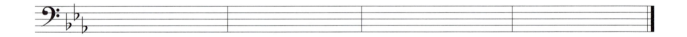

5. Adagio

Melodic Dictation: QUIZ NO. 2

Animato

1.

Comodo

2.

Allegro

3.

Cantabile

4.

Allegro con brio

5.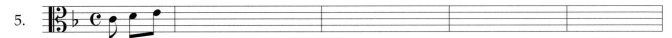

Melodic Dictation: QUIZ NO. 3

Andante

1.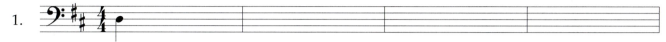

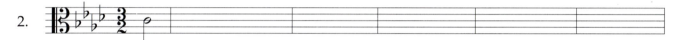

Cantabile

2.

Allegretto

3.

Piacevole

4.

5.

Passionato

Harmonic Dictation: The supertonic triad; Inversions of V7

Basic Progressions

Supertonic triad

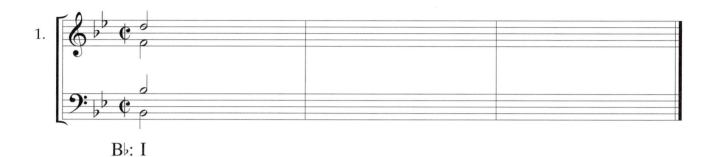

1.

Bb: I

2.

b: i

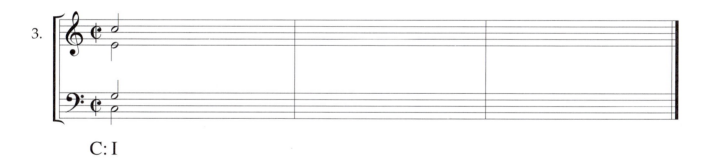

3.

C: I

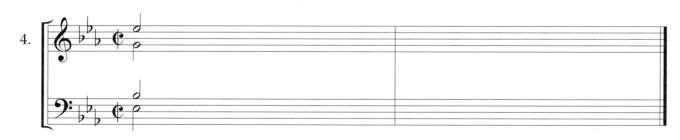

4.

Eb: I

5.

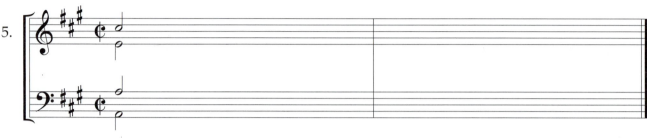

A: I

6.

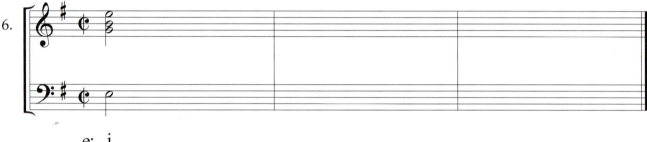

e: i

7.

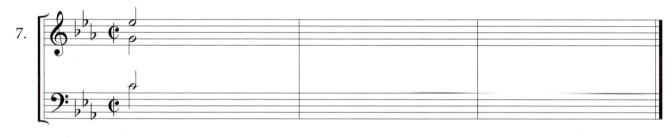

c: i

8.

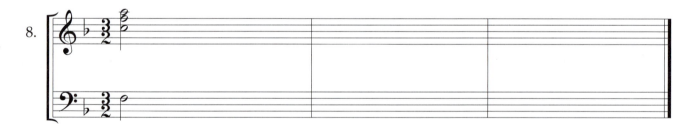

F: I

9.

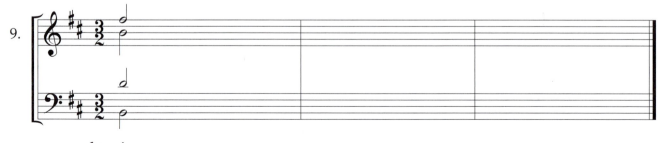

b: i

Inversions of V7

10.

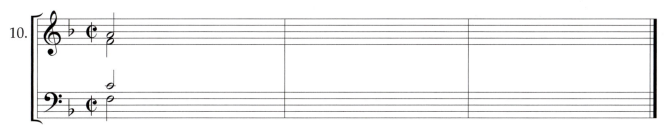

F: I

11.

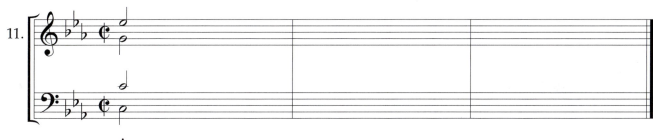

c: i

12.

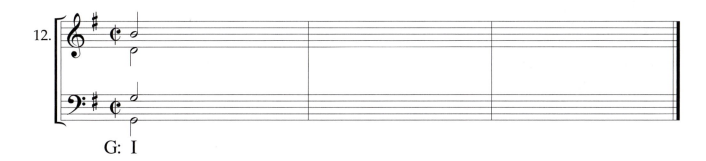

G: I

13.

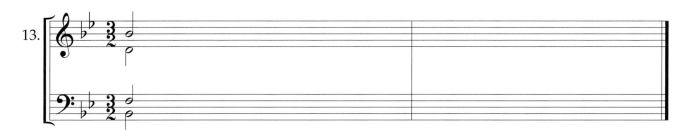

B♭: I

14.

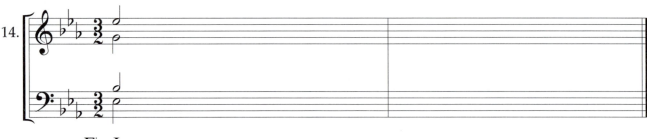

E♭: I

15.

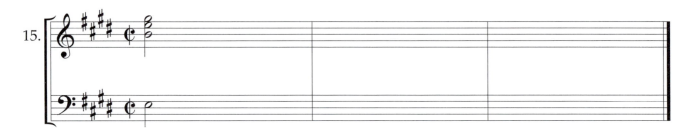

E: I

16.

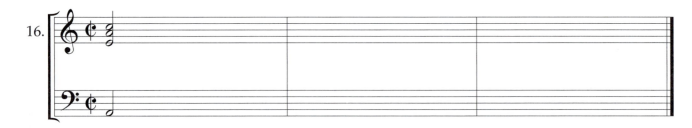

a: i

17.

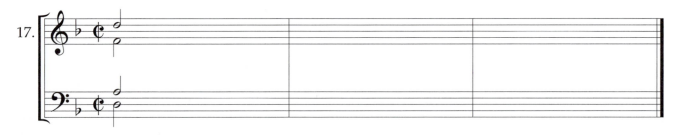

d: i

18.

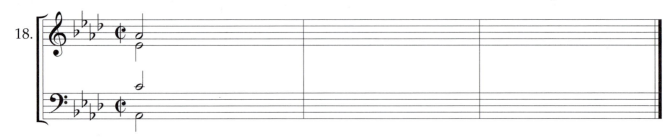

A♭: I

Phrase-length Exercises

1.
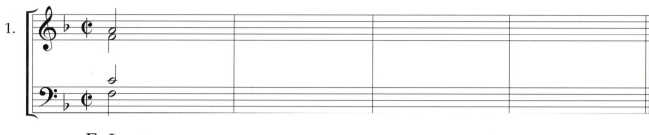

F: I

2.
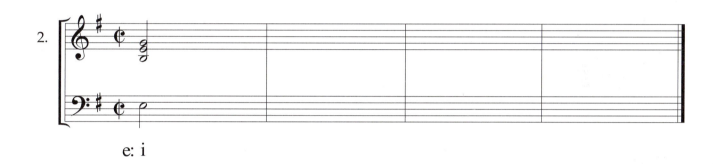

e: i

3.
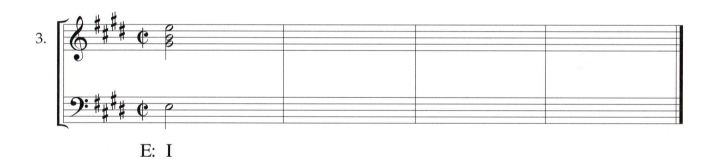

E: I

4.
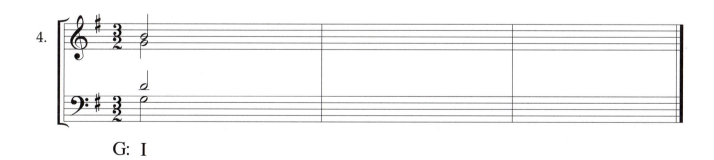

G: I

5.

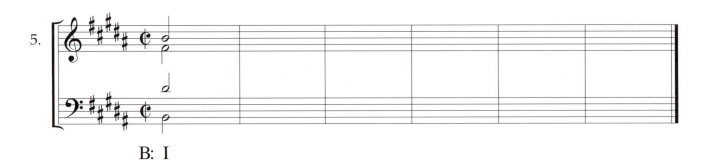

B: I

6.

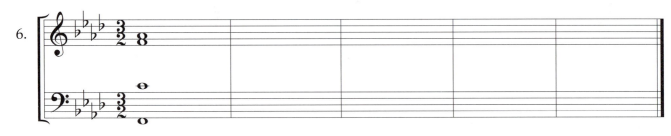

f: i

7.

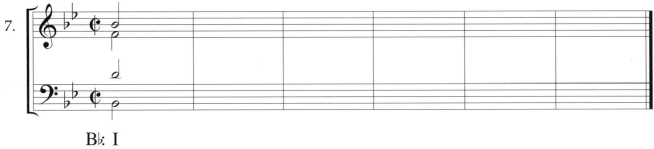

B♭: I

8.

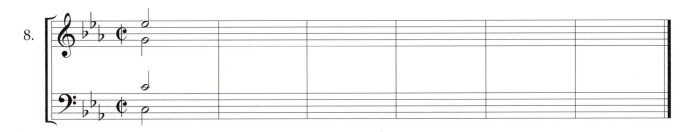

c: i

9.

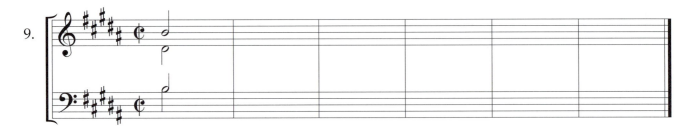

B: I

10.

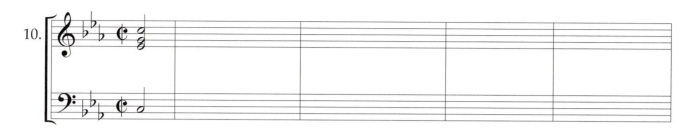

c: i

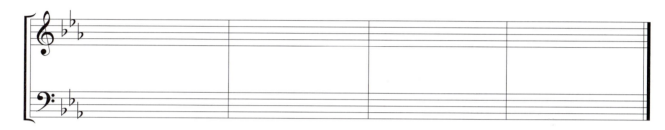

11.

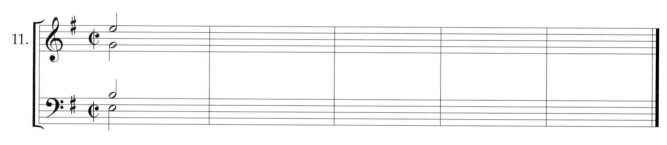

e: i

12.

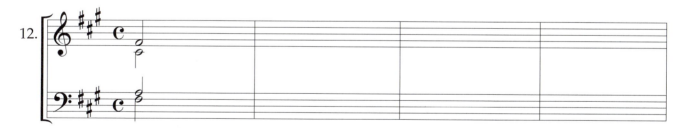

f♯: i

Harmonic Dictation: QUIZ NO. 1

1.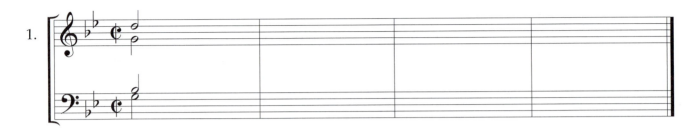

  g: i

2.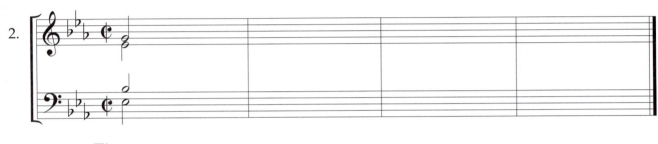

  E♭: I

3.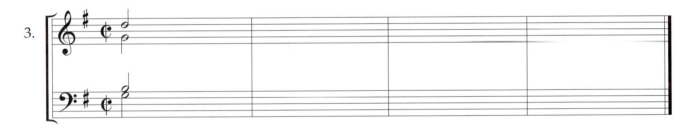

  G: I

4.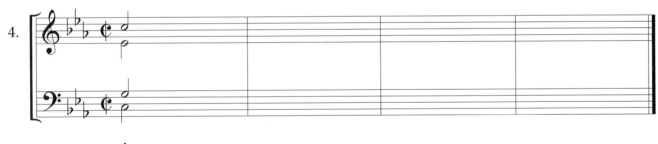

  c: i

5.

E: I

Harmonic Dictation: QUIZ NO. 2

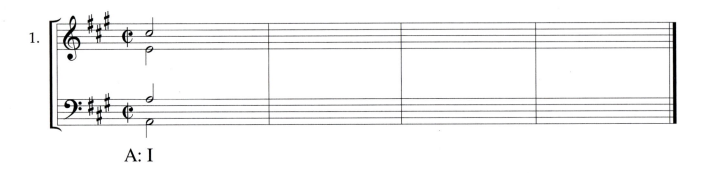

1.

A: I

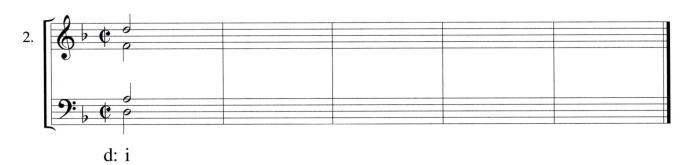

2.

d: i

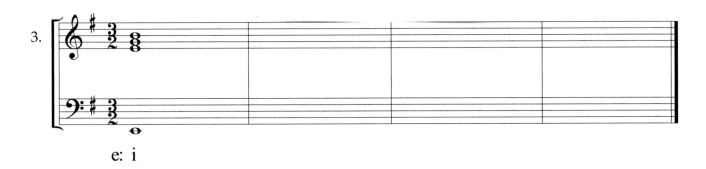

3.

e: i

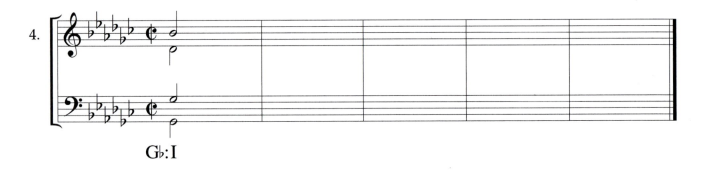

4.

G♭: I

5.
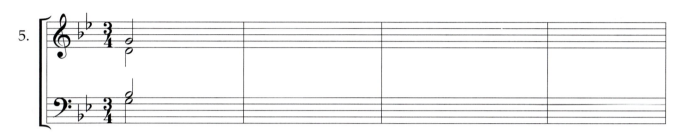

g: i

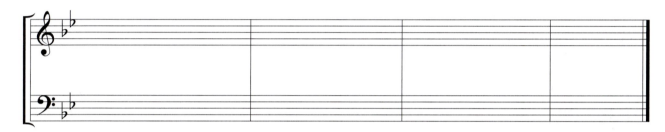

Class: _____

Name: _____

Professor: _____

Harmonic Dictation: QUIZ NO. 3

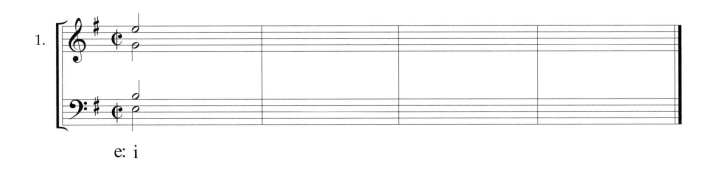

1.

e: i

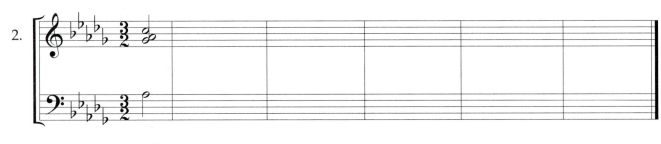

2.

D♭: V⁷

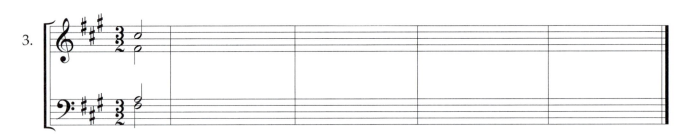

3.

f♯: i

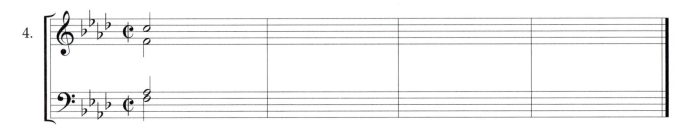

4.

f: i

5.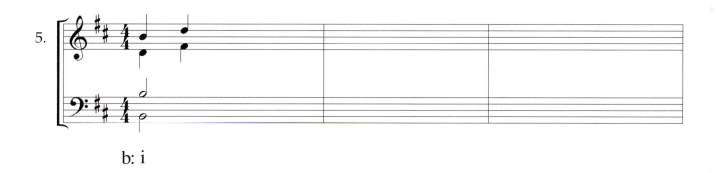

b: i

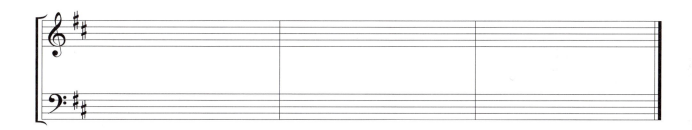

Unit 8

Rhythmic Dictation: Compound meter

1.  $\frac{6}{8}$

2. 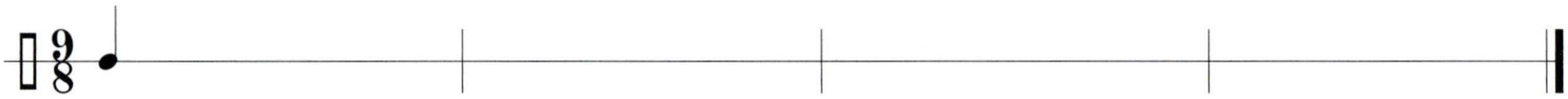 $\frac{9}{8}$

3.  $\frac{6}{8}$

4.  $\frac{9}{8}$

5. $\frac{6}{4}$

6. $\frac{12}{8}$

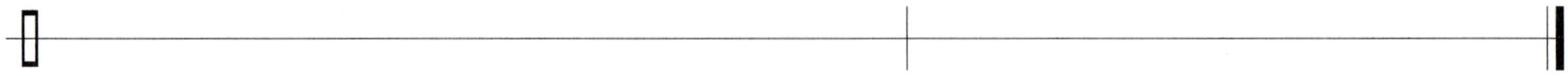

7.

8.

9.

10.

11.

12.

13.

14.

15.

16.

Rhythmic Dictation: QUIZ NO. 3

1.

2.

3.

4.

5.

Melodic Dictation: All diatonic triads

Preliminary Exercises

1.

2.

3.

4.

5.

6.

7.

8.

9.

10.

Melodies

Grazioso

1.

Allegretto

2.

Moderato

3.

Andante

4.

Religioso

5.

Allegro, ma non troppo

6.

Animato

7.

Andantino

8.

Flowing

9.

10.

Moderato

11.

Andante   (after Mendelssohn)

12.

Gigue   (after J.S. Bach)

Melodic Dictation: QUIZ NO. 1

Moderato

1.

Allegro, ma non troppo

2.

Lento

3.

Andante

4.

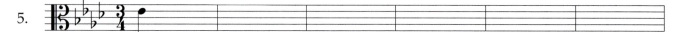

Con anima

5.

Melodic Dictation: QUIZ NO. 2

Moderato

1.

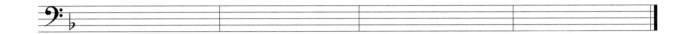

Giocoso

2.

Menuetto

3.

4. Adagio

5. Moderato

Melodic Dictation: QUIZ NO. 3

Brightly

1.

Adagio

2.

Moderato

3.

Cantabile

4.

Tempo di Valse

5.

Harmonic Dictation: All diatonic triads

Basic Progressions

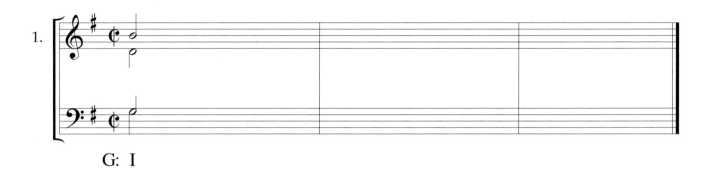

1. G: I

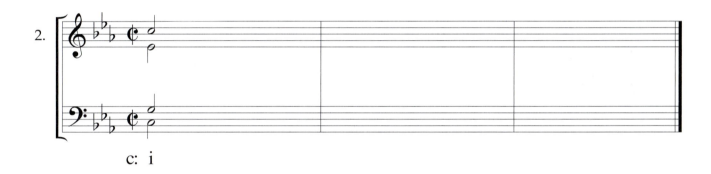

2. c: i

3. B: I

4. e♭: i

5.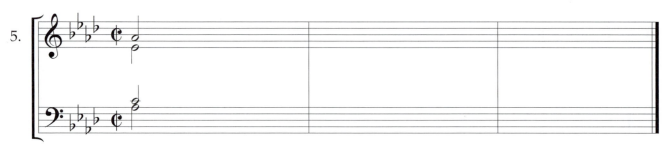

    A♭: I

6.

    b: i

7.

    F: I

8.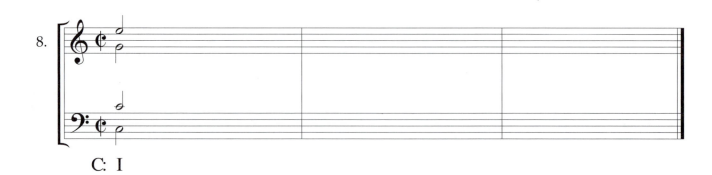

    C: I

9.

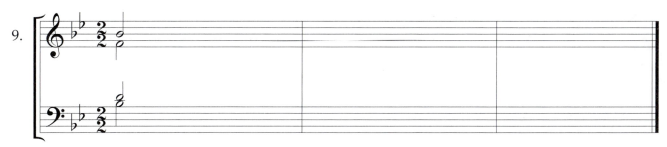

Bb: I

10.

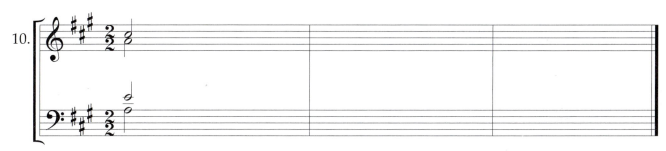

A: I

11.

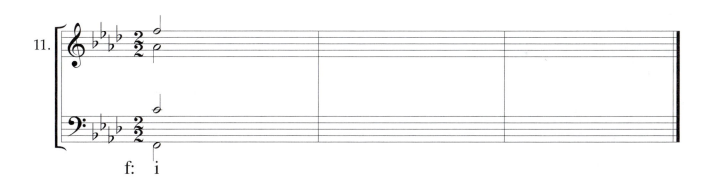

f: i

12.

C: I

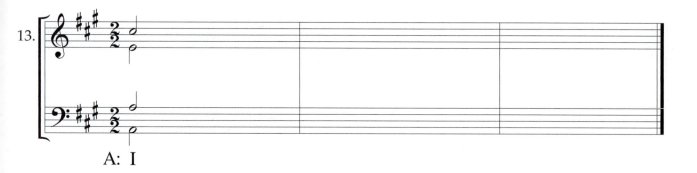

A: I

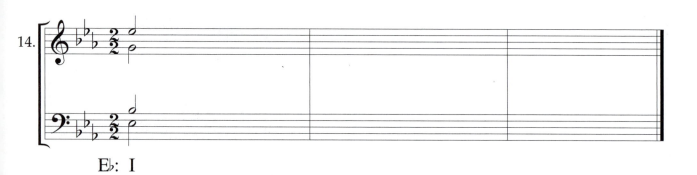

E♭: I

b: i

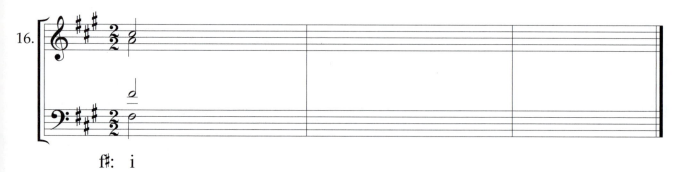

f♯: i

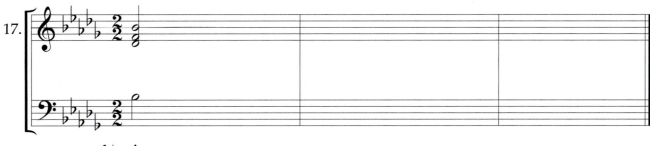

b♭: i

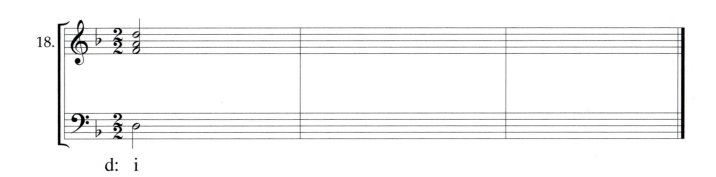

d: i

Phrase-length Exercises

1.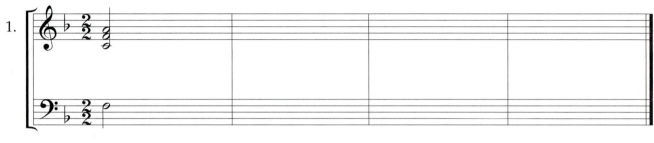

F: I

2.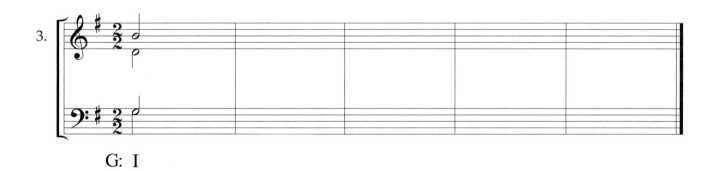

e: i

3.

G: I

4.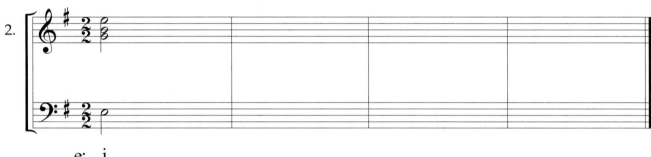

F: I

5.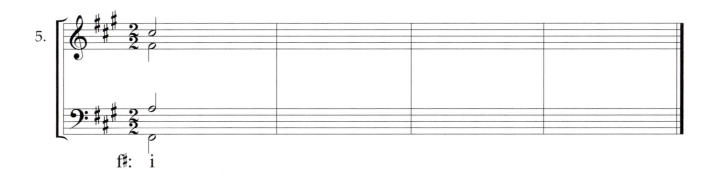

f#:   i

6.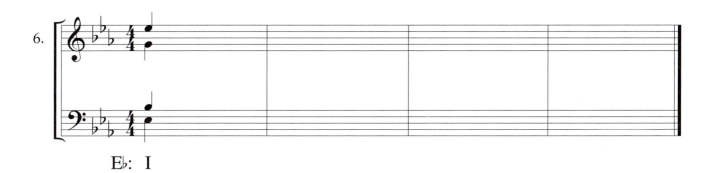

Eb: I

7.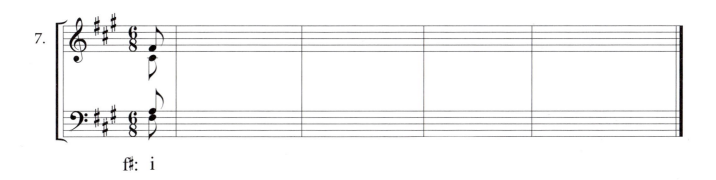

f#:   i

8.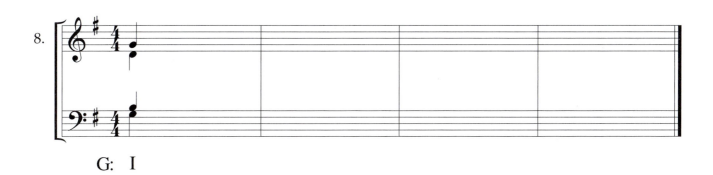

G: I

9.

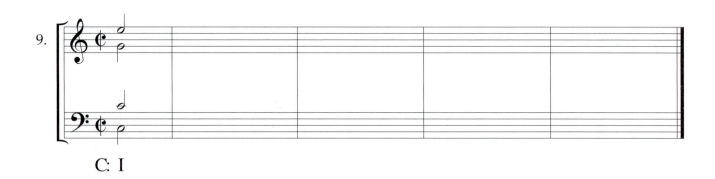

C: I

10.

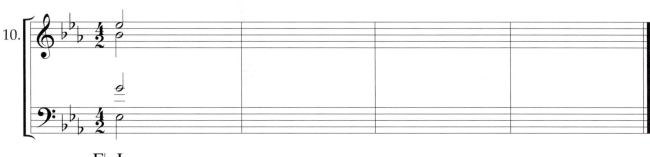

E♭: I

Harmonic Dictation: QUIZ NO. 1

1.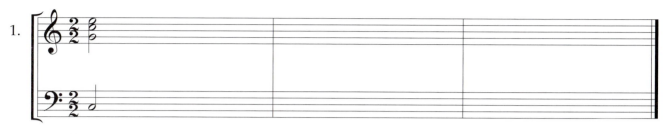

C: I

2.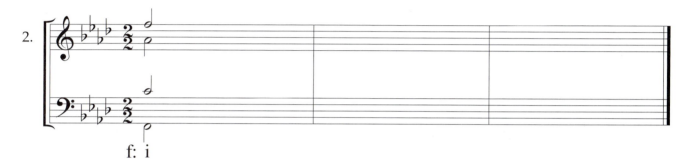

f: i

3.

D: I

4.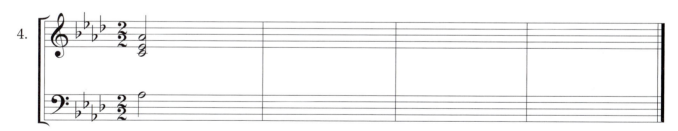

A♭ : I

5.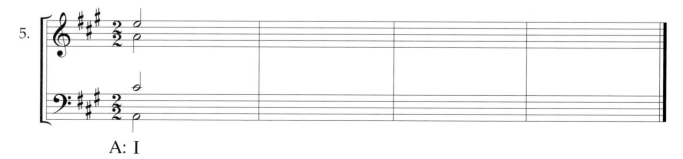

A: I

Harmonic Dictation: QUIZ NO. 2

1.

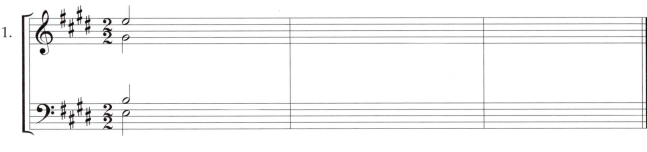

E: I

2.

f: i

3.

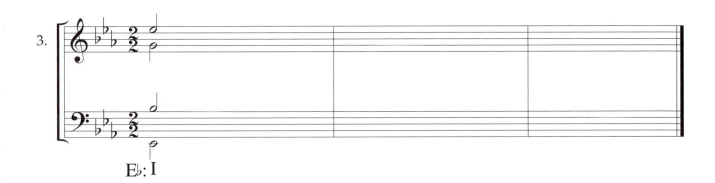

E♭: I

4.

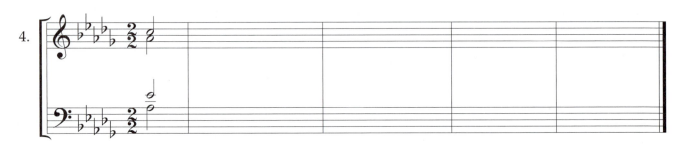

D♭: V

5.

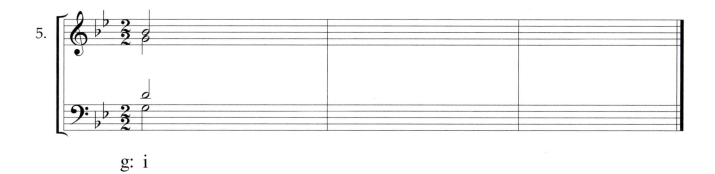

g: i

Class: _____   Name: _____

Professor: _____

Harmonic Dictation: QUIZ NO. 3

1.
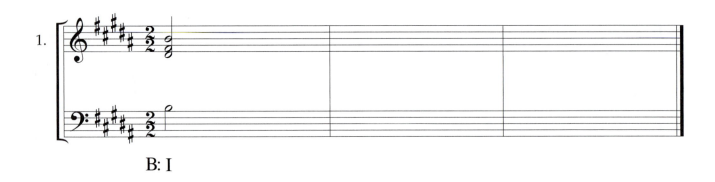

B: I

2.
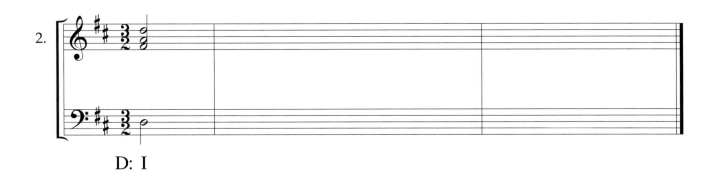

D: I

3.
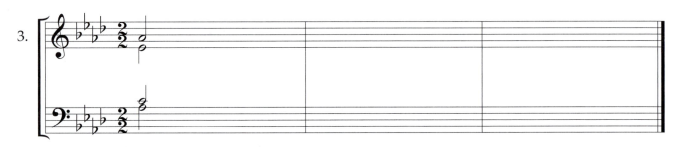

A♭: I

4.
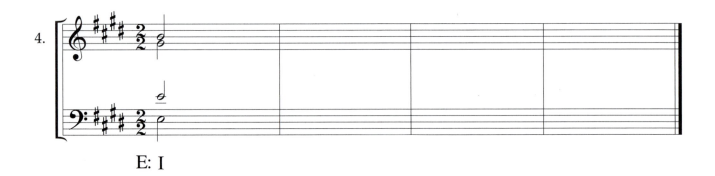

E: I

200   Unit 8

5.

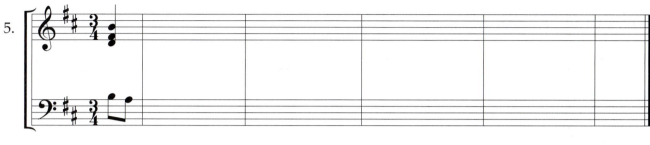

b: i

Unit 9

Rhythmic Dictation: Triplets

1. $\frac{2}{4}$

2. $\frac{3}{4}$

3. $\frac{2}{4}$

4. $\frac{3}{4}$

5. $\frac{2}{4}$

6.

7.

8.

9.

10.

11.

12.

This example begins with an upbeat.

13.

14.

15.

16.

Melodies

1.

2.

3.

4.

Teneramente

5.

Lento

6.

Cantabile

7.

Moderato

8.

9.

Grazioso

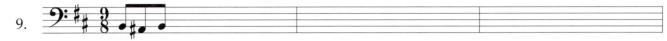

10.

Ruhig

11.

Moderato

Risoluto

12.

Cantabile

13.

Dolore

14.

Andante espressivo

15.

16.

Melodic Dictation: QUIZ NO. 1

Allegretto

1.

Andantino

2.

Moderato

3.

Andante

4.

Andante espressivo

5.

Melodic Dictation: QUIZ NO. 2

Moderato

1.

Lively

2.

Con moto

3.

Cantabile

4.

Allegro piacevole

5.

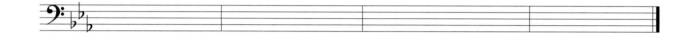

Melodic Dictation: QUIZ NO. 3

1. Marziale

2. Moderato

3. Allegro non troppo

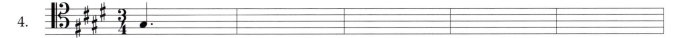

4. Comodo

Amoroso

5.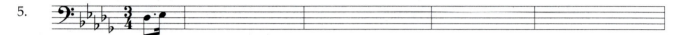

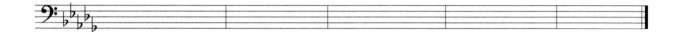

Harmonic Dictation: Supertonic and leading tone sevenths

Basic Progressions

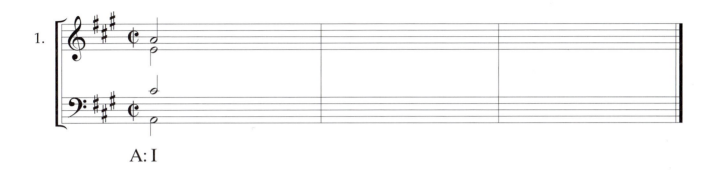

1. A: I

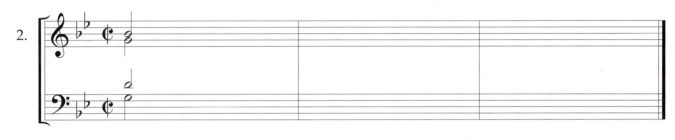

2. g: i

3. C: I

4. g♯: i

5.

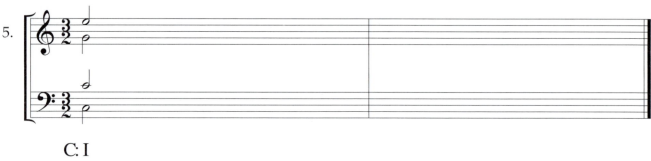

C: I

6.

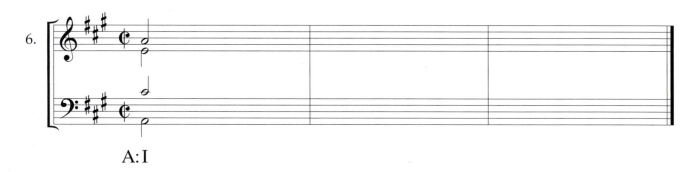

A: I

7.

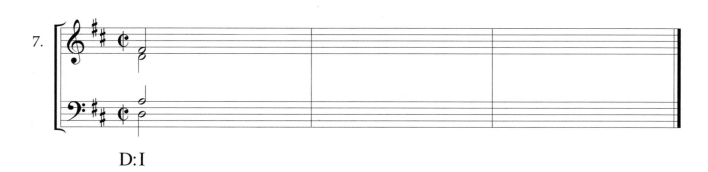

D: I

8.

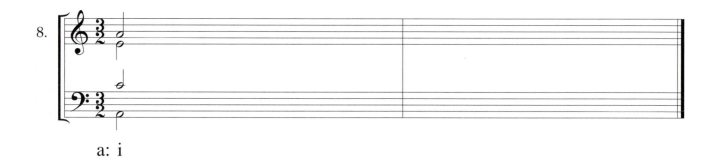

a: i

9.

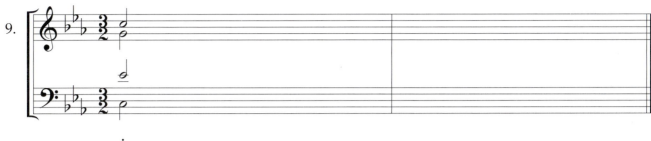

c: i

10.

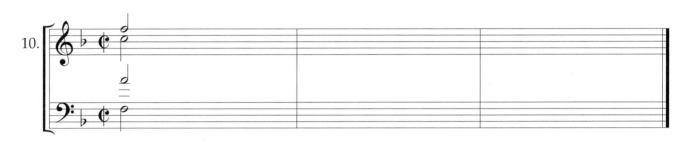

F: I

11.

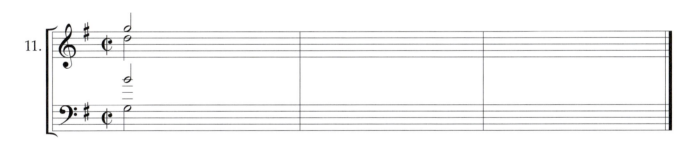

G: I

12.

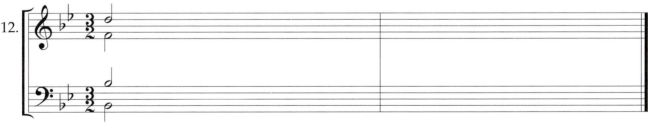

B♭: I

13.

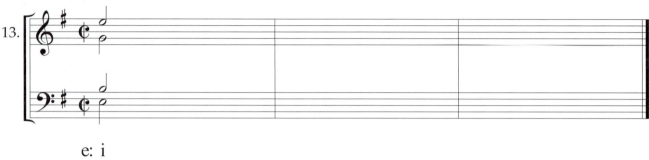

e: i

14.

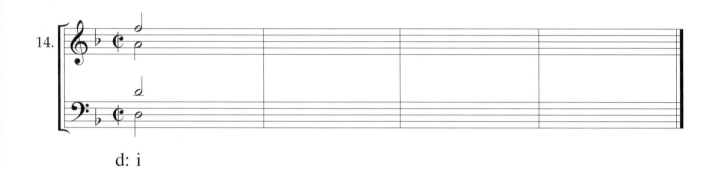

d: i

15.

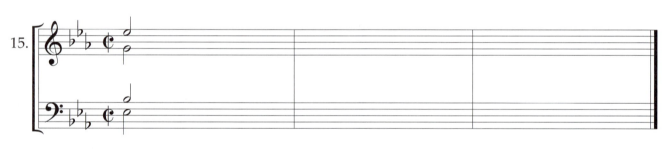

E♭: I

16.

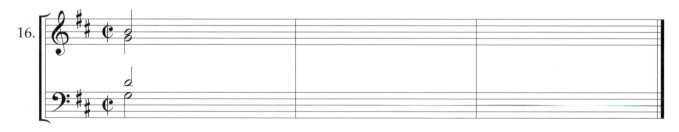

D: IV

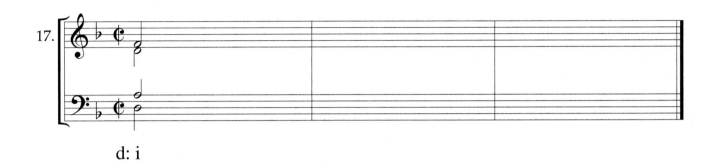

d: i

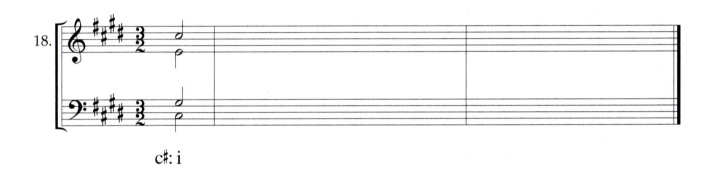

c#: i

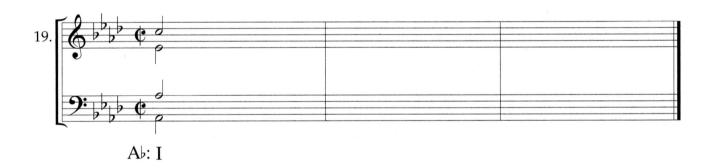

A♭: I

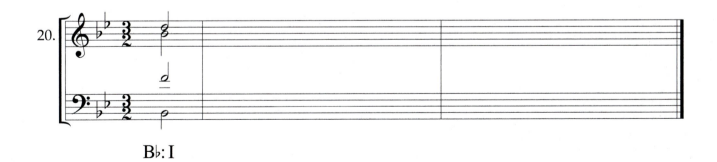

B♭: I

Phrase-length Exercises

1.

b: i

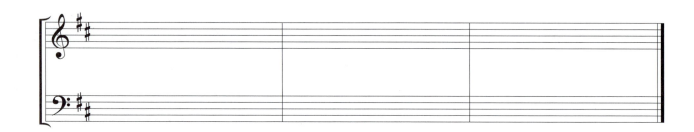

2.
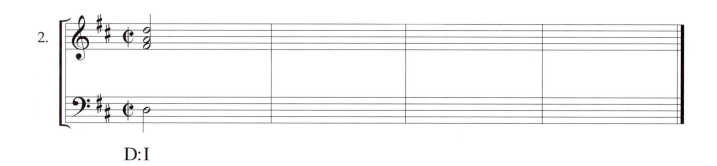

D: I

3.
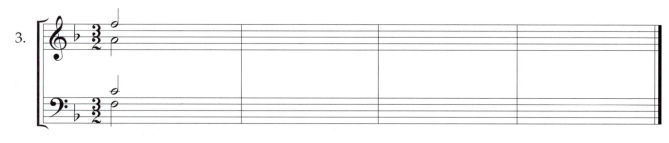

F: I

4.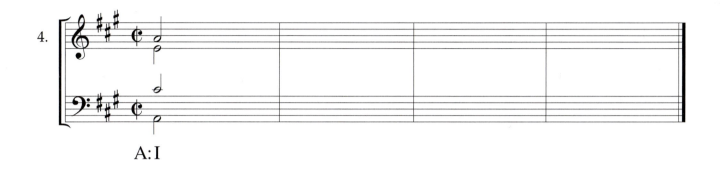

A: I

5.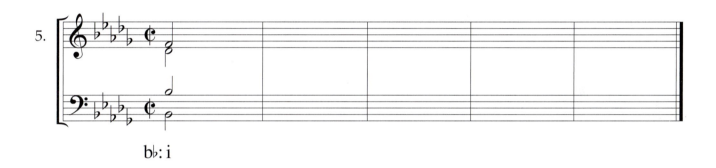

b♭: i

6.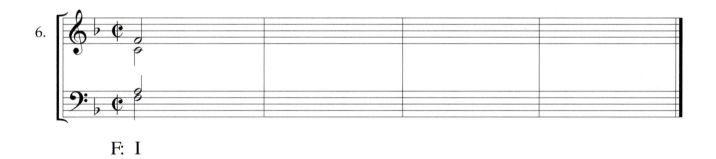

F: I

7.

f♯: i

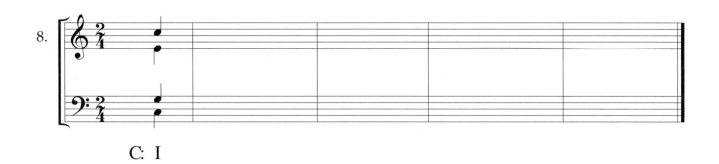

C: I

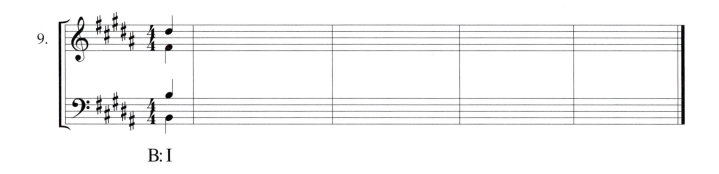

B: I

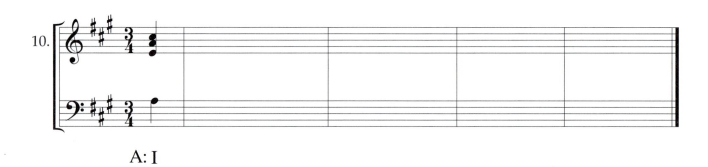

A: I

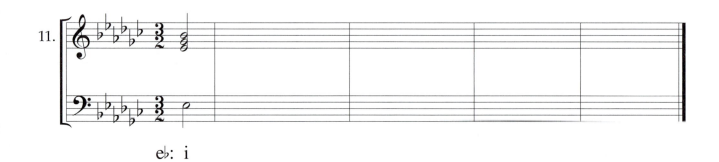

e♭: i

12.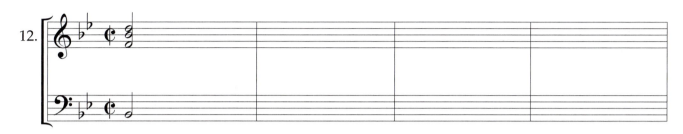

B♭:   I

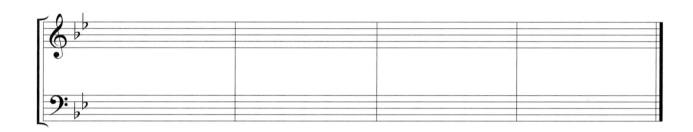

Harmonic Dictation: QUIZ NO. 1

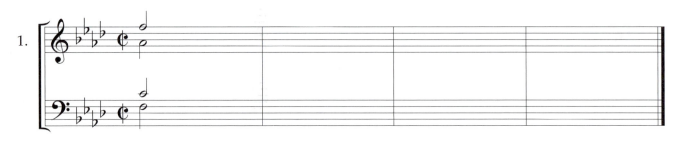

1.   f: i

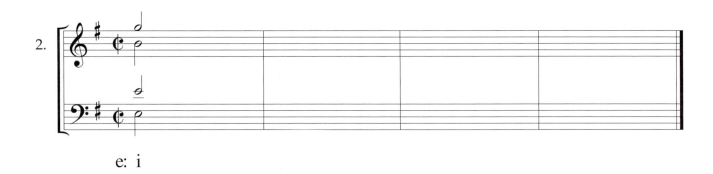

2.   e: i

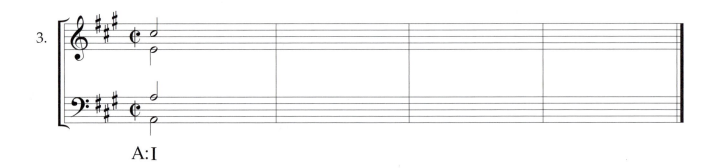

3.   A: I

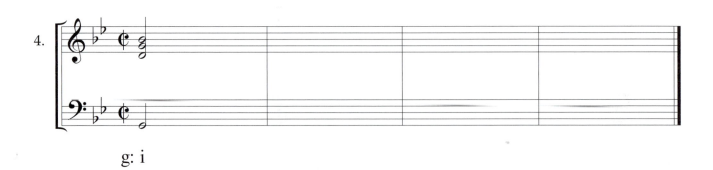

4.   g: i

5.

E: I

Harmonic Dictation: QUIZ NO. 2

1.
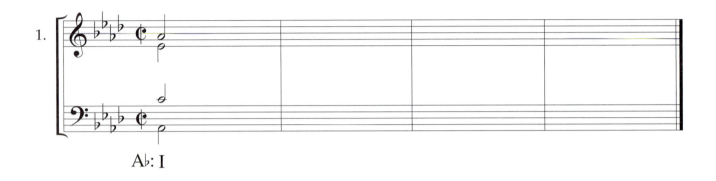

Ab: I

2.
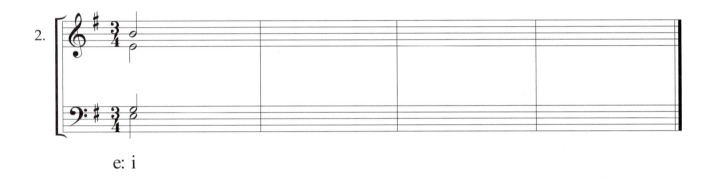

e: i

3.
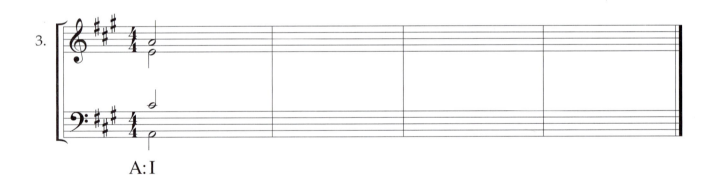

A: I

4.
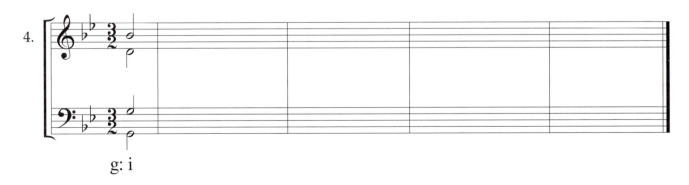

g: i

5.

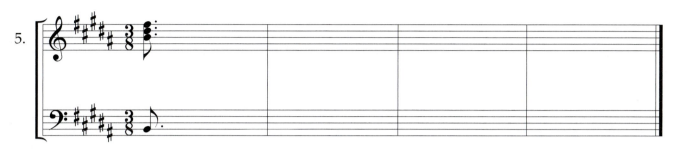

B: I

Class: _____   Name: _____

Professor: _____

Harmonic Dictation: QUIZ NO. 3

1.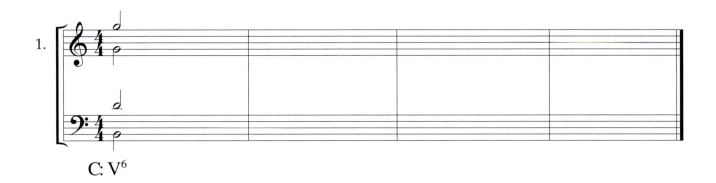

    C: V⁶

2.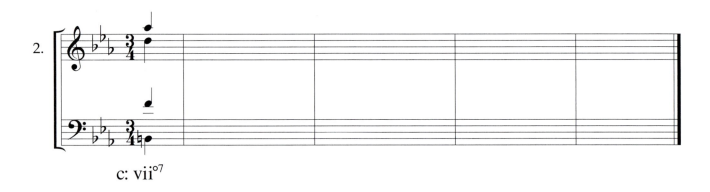

    c: vii°⁷

3.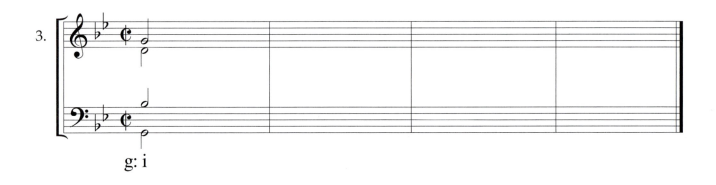

    g: i

4.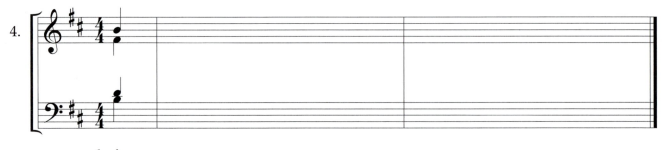

    b: i

5.

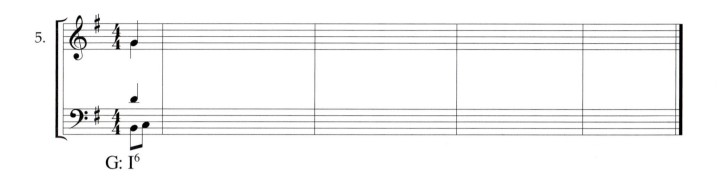

G: I⁶

Unit 10

Examples from Music Literature

1. Johann Sebastian Bach. Minuet in G

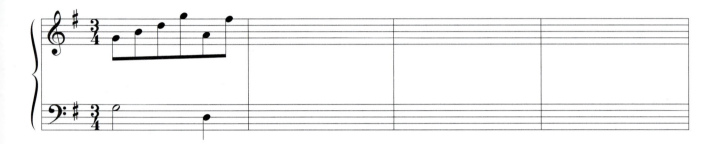

2. Johann Sebastian Bach. *Aus meines Herzens Grunde* (chorale)

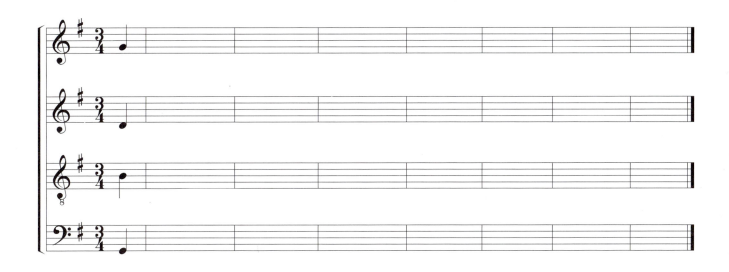

3. Johann Sebastian Bach. *Wir glauben all' an einen Gott* (chorale)

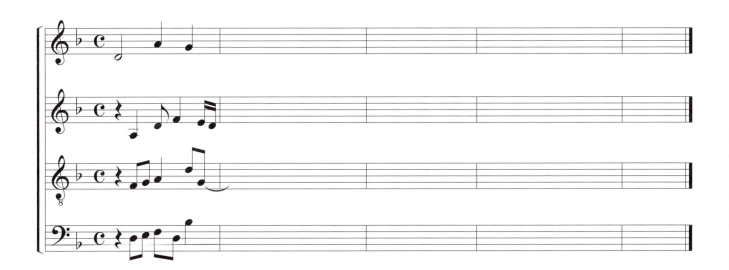

4. Ludwig van Beethoven. Six Variations on *Nel cor più non mi sento*

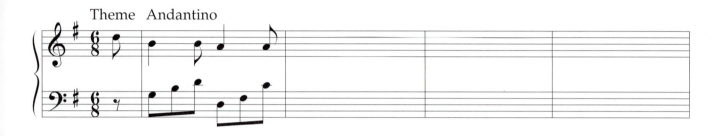

5. Friedrich Kuhlau. Sonatina Op. 88, No. 3, Mvt. III

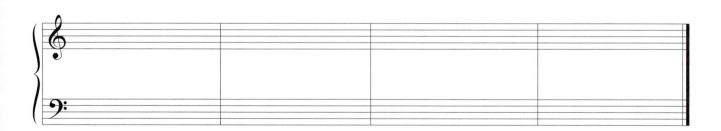

6. Wolfgang Amadeus Mozart. String Quintet, K. 581, Mvt. IV

QUIZ NO. 1

Joseph Haydn. Sonata in D Major, Hob. XVI:33, Menuetto con Variazioni

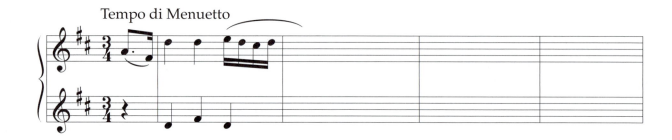

QUIZ NO. 2

John Farmer. *Fair Phyllis* (chorale)

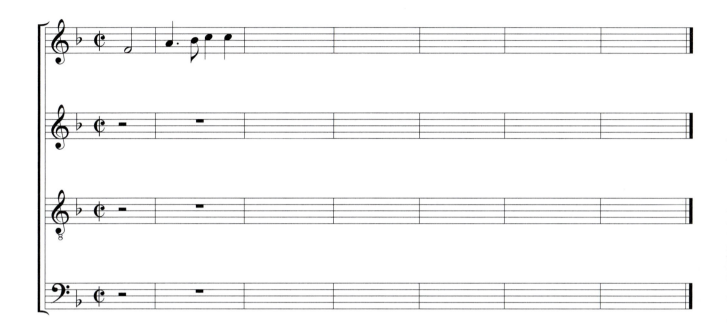

QUIZ NO. 3

Wolfgang Amadeus Mozart. String Quartet, K. 80, Mvt. III, Trio

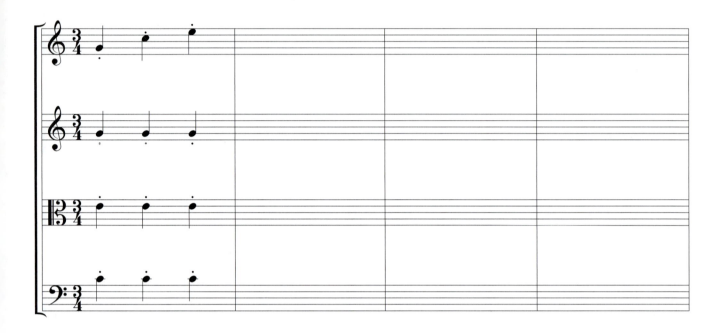

Unit 11

Rhythmic Dictation: Syncopation

1.

Countoff begins on the downbeat of the incomplete measure.

2.

3.

4.

5.

6.

7.

8.

9.

10.

11.

12.

13.

14.

Rhythmic Dictation: QUIZ NO. 1

1.

2.

3.

4.

5.

Class:

Name: _____

Professor:

Rhythmic Dictation: QUIZ NO. 2

1.

2.

3.

4.

5.

Rhythmic Dictation: QUIZ NO. 3

1.

Countoff begins on the downbeat of the incomplete measure.

2.

3.

4.

5.

Melodic Dictation: Non-dominant seventh chords

Preliminary Exercises

1. (bass clef, 2 sharps, common time)

2. (treble clef, 2 flats, 3/4)

3. (treble clef, 2 sharps, 2/4)

4. (bass clef, 9/8)

5. (treble clef, 2 flats, 3/4)

6. (bass clef, 1 sharp, common time)

Melodies

Not fast

1.

Cantabile

2.

Giocoso

3.

Comodo

4.

5. **Marziale**

6. **Cantabile**

7. **Grazioso**

8. **Con brio**

Gently

9.

Moderato

10.

Andante

11.

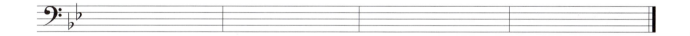

Lento

12.

Allegro ma non troppo

13.

Deliberamente

14.

Allegretto

15.

Amoroso

16.

Melodic Dictation: QUIZ NO. 1

1. Grazioso

2. Andante espressivo

3. Ragtime

4. Andantino

5. Moderato

Melodic Dictation: QUIZ NO. 2

1. Cantabile

2. Sea chanty

3. Energico

4. Largo

Giocoso

5.

Melodic Dictation: QUIZ NO. 3

Moderato

1.

Molto espressivo

2.

Giocoso

3.

Molto cantabile

4.

Habanera

5.

Harmonic Dictation: Non-dominant seventh chords

Basic Progressions

1.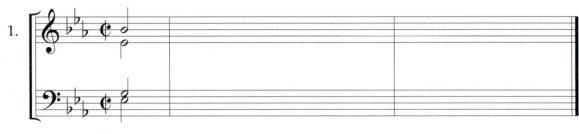

      Eb: I

2.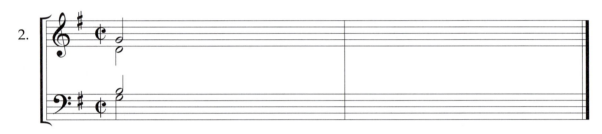

      G: I

3.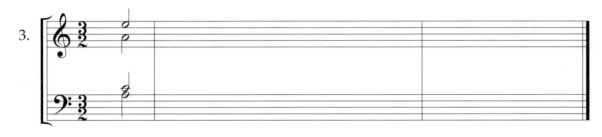

      a: i

4.

      f: i

5.

B: I

6.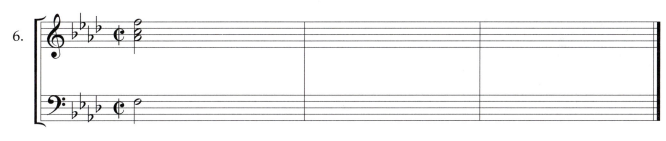

f: i

7.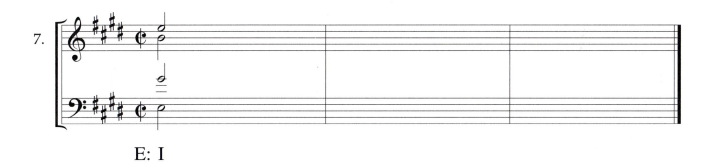

E: I

8.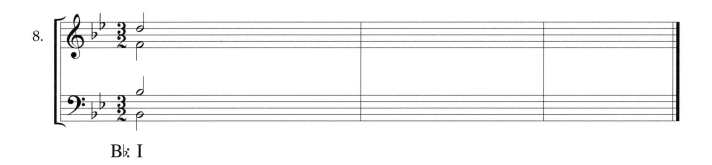

B♭: I

9.

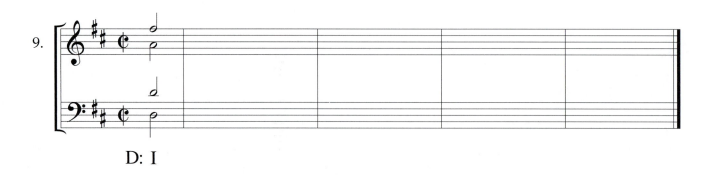

D: I

10.

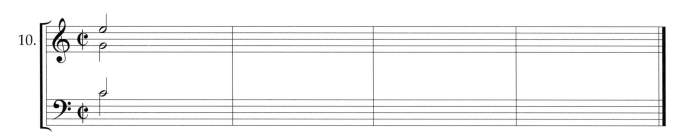

C: I

Phrase-length Exercises

1.

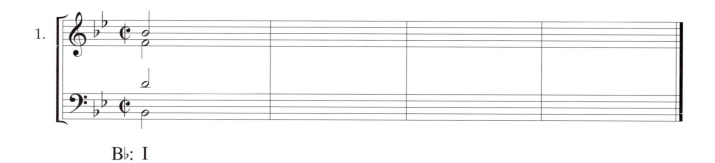

Bb: I

2.

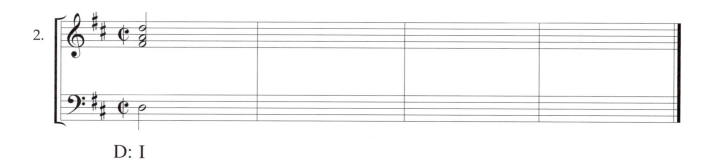

D: I

3.

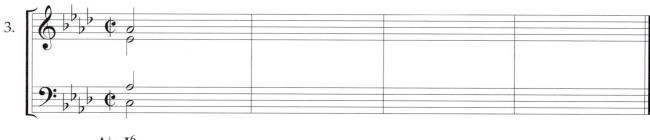

Ab: I^6

4.

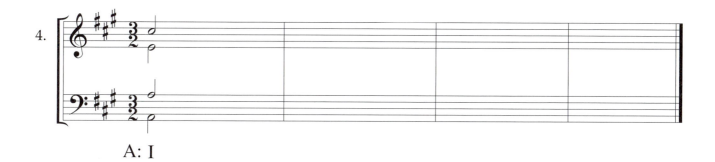

A: I

Class: _____   **Name:** _____

Professor: _____

5.

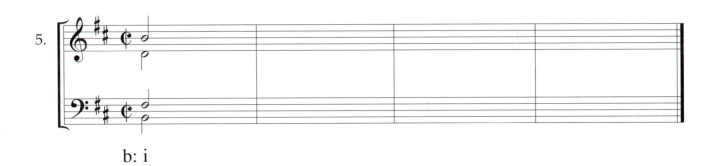

b: i

6.

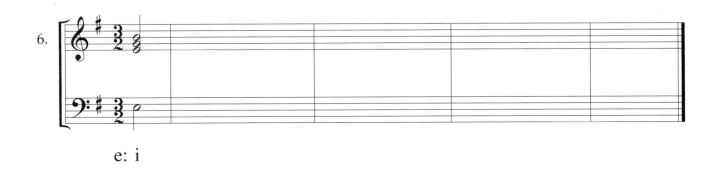

e: i

7.

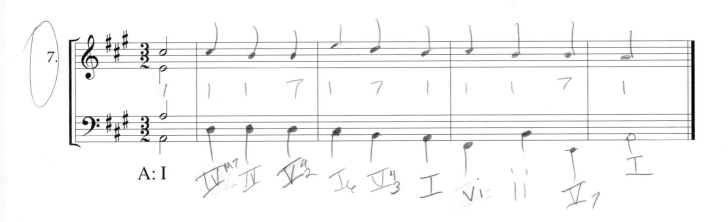

A: I   IV^{M7} IV V$^4_2$ I$_6$ V$^4_3$ I   vi: ii   V$_7$ I

8.

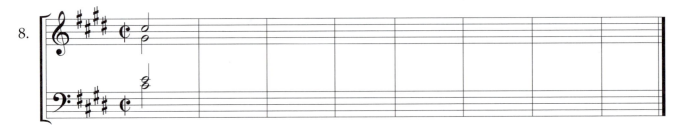

c#: i

262

Unit 11

5.

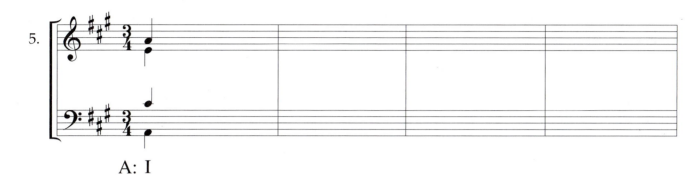

A: I

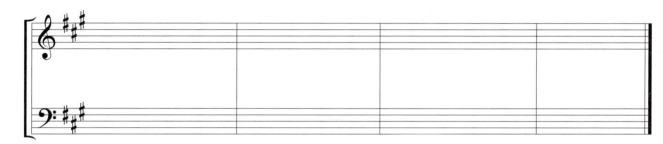

Harmonic Dictation: QUIZ NO. 3

1.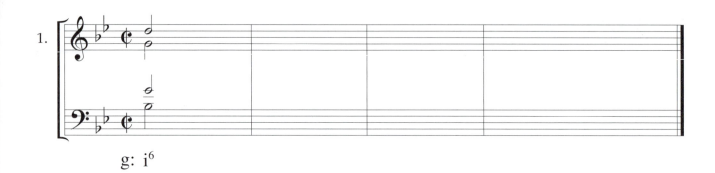

g: i⁶

2.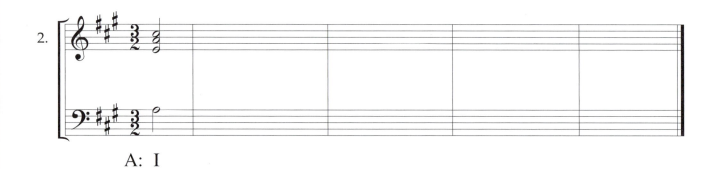

A: I

3.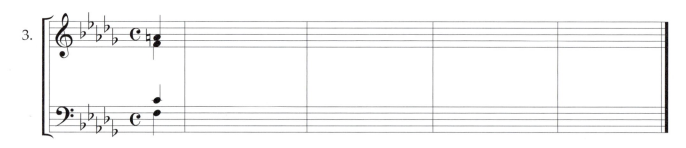

b♭: V♮

4.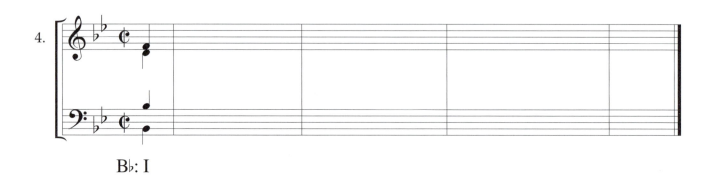

B♭: I

5.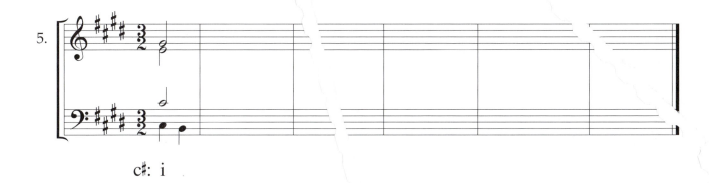

c#: i

Unit 12 ━━━━━━━━━━━━━━━━━━━━━━━━━

Melodic Dictation: Scalar variants, modal borrowing, decorative chromaticism

Preliminary Exercises

Scalar variants

1.

2.

3.

4.

5.

6.

7.

8.

Modal borrowing

9.

10.

11.

12.

13.

14.

15.

16.

Decorative chromaticism

17.

18.

19.

20.

21.

22.

23.

24.

25.

26.

Melodies

1.

Cantabile

2.

Andante

3.

Doloroso

4.

Amoroso

5.

Grazioso

Andantino

6.

Deliberamente

7.

Con moto

8.

Giovale

9.

Moderato

10.

Marziale

11.

Con moto

12.

Allegro ma non troppo

13.

Giocoso

14.

Andantino

15.

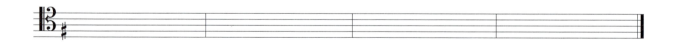

5.

Class: _____

Name: _____

Professor: _____

Melodic Dictation: QUIZ NO. 2

Lento

1.

Spiritoso

2.

Amabile

3.

Con anima

4.

Harmonic Dictation: Scalar variants, modal borrowing

Basic Progressions

Scalar variants

1.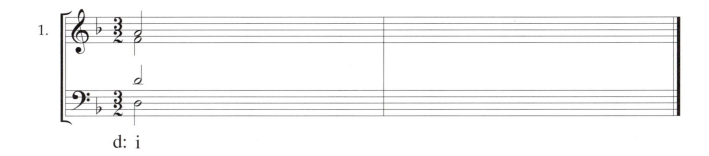

d: i

2.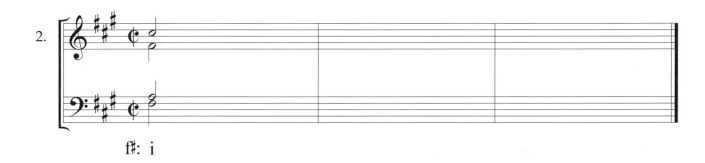

f♯: i

3.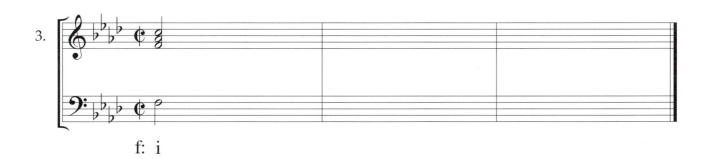

f: i

4.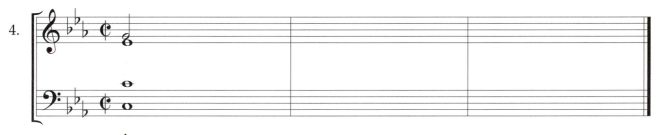

c: i

5.

e: i

6.

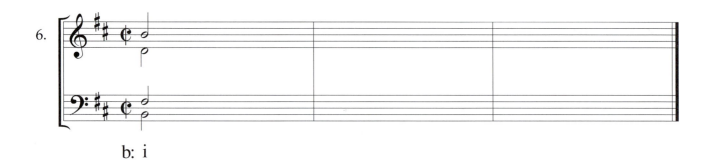

b: i

7.

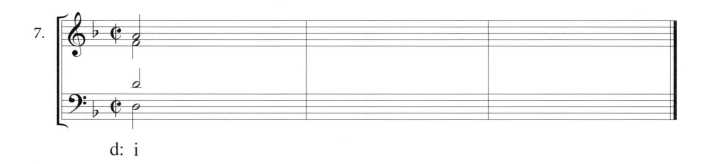

d: i

8.

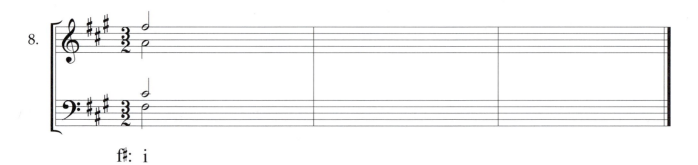

f♯: i

9.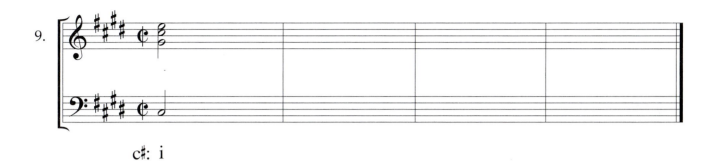

c#: i

10.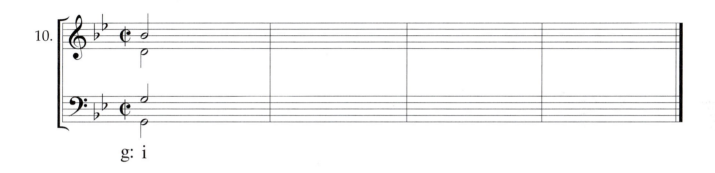

g: i

Modal borrowing

11.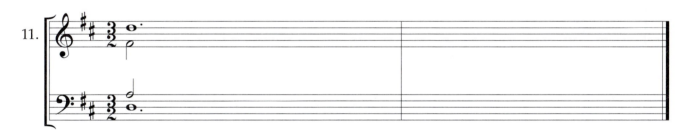

D: I

12.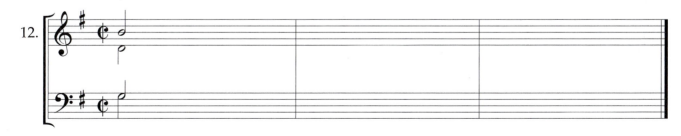

G: I

Eb: I

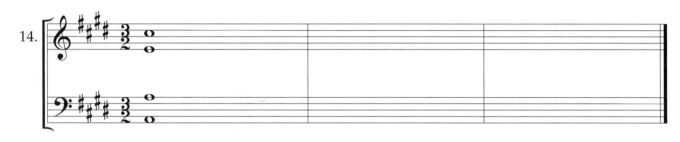

E: IV

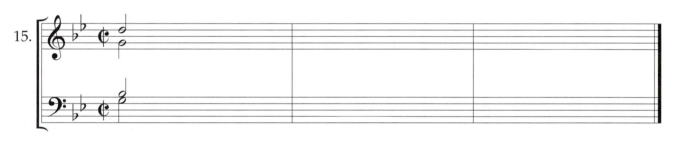

g: i

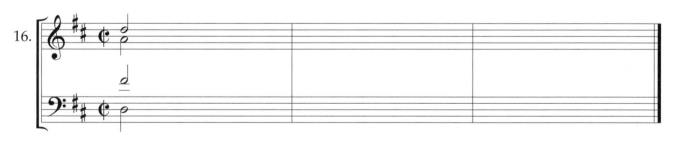

D: I

Class: _____ Name: _____

Professor: _____

17.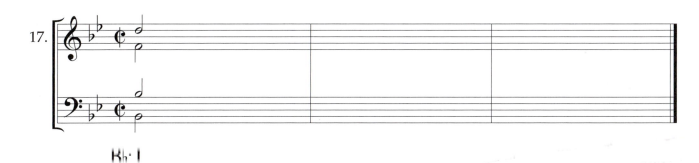

B♭: I

18.

A: I

19.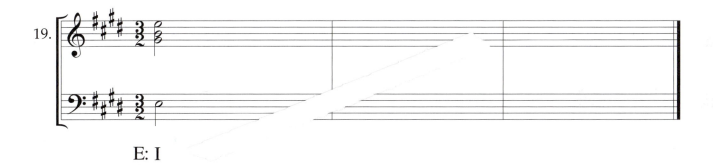

E: I

20.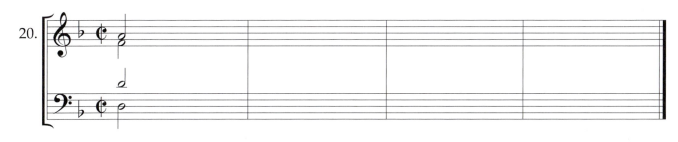

d: i

Phrase-length Exercises

1.

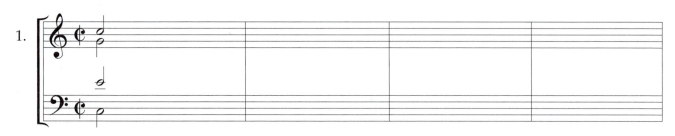

G: I

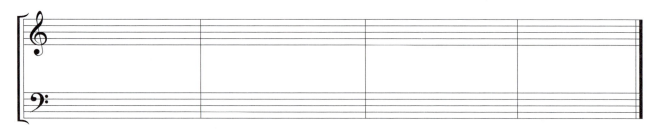

2.

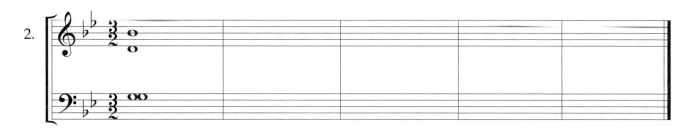

g: i

3.

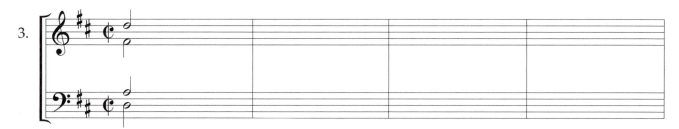

D: I

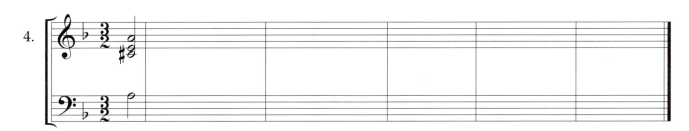

d: V♯

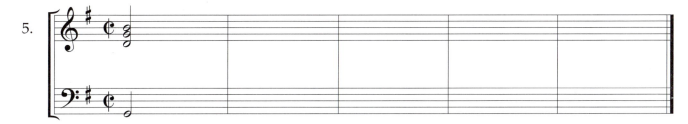

G: I

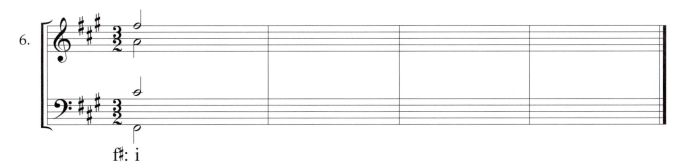

f♯: i

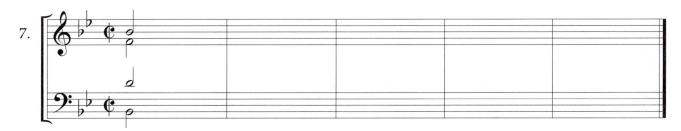

B♭: I

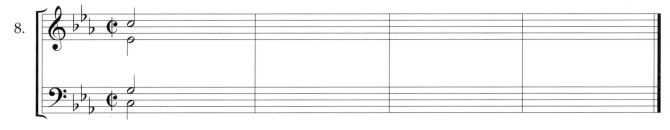

c: i

9.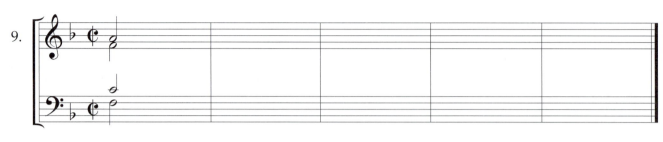

F: I

10.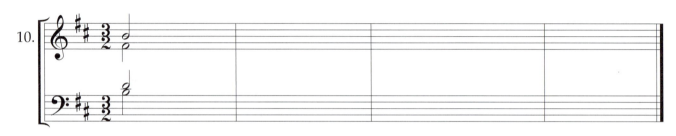

b: i

11.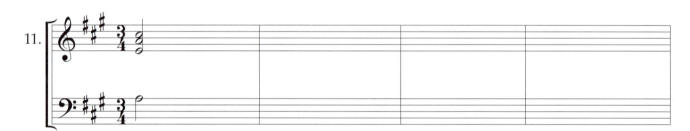

A: I

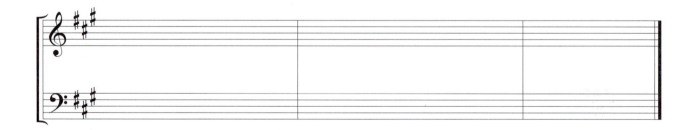

12.

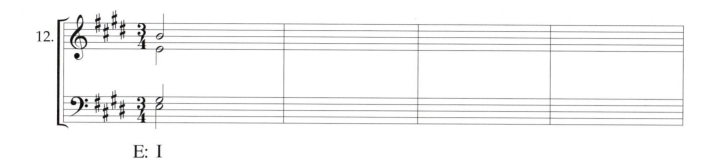

E: I

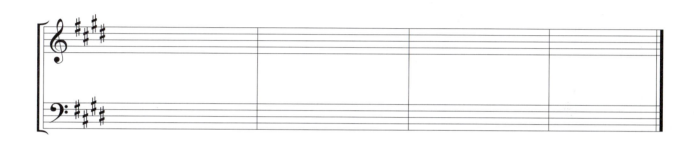

13.

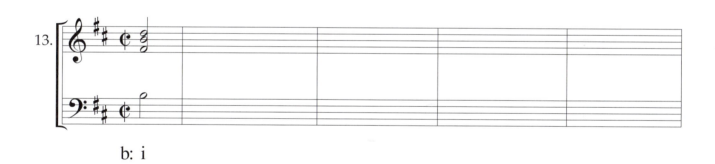

b: i

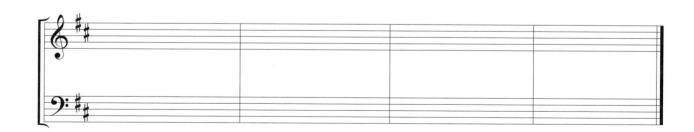

14.

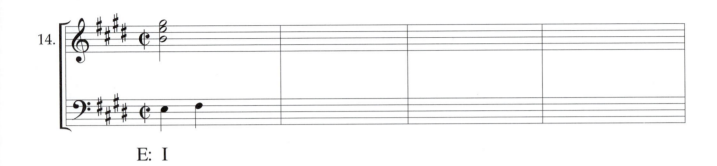

E: I

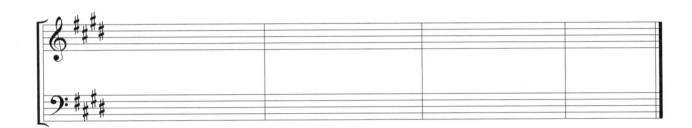

Harmonic Dictation: QUIZ NO. 3

1.

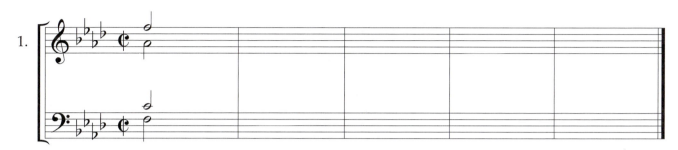

f: i

2.

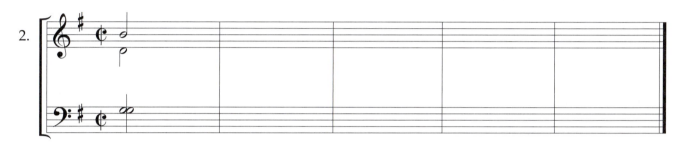

G: I

3.

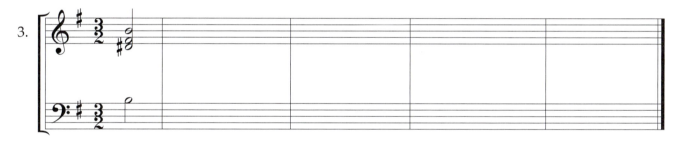

e: V♯

4.

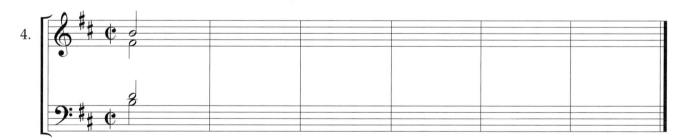

b: i

5.

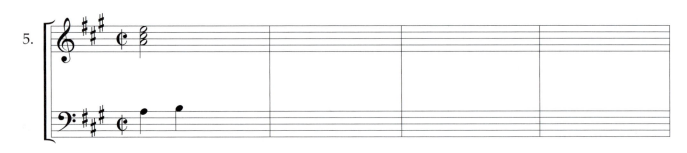

A: I

Unit 13

Melodic Dictation: Secondary dominants

Preliminary Exercises

1.

2.

3.

4.

5.

6.

7.

8.

9.

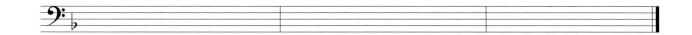

10.

Melodies

Allegro

1.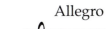

Moderato

2.

Cantabile

3.

Spiritoso

4.

Piacevole

5.

Allegretto

6.

Adagio

7.

Grazioso

8.

Andantino

9.

Allegro ma non troppo

10.

Gigue

11.

Siciliano

12.

Eroico

13.

Allegretto

14.

5.

Melodic Dictation: QUIZ NO. 3

1.

Allegretto

2.

Andantino

3.

Moderato

4.

Amabile

Giocoso

5.

Harmonic Dictation: Secondary dominants

Basic Progressions

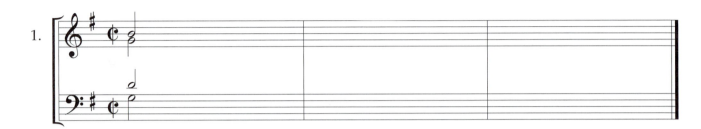

1.

G: I

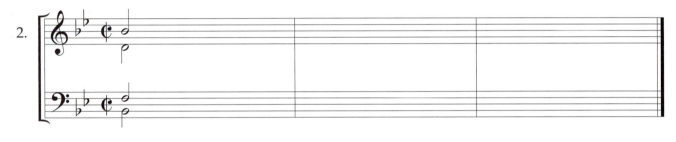

2.

B♭: I

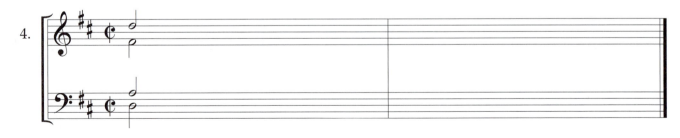

3.

c: i

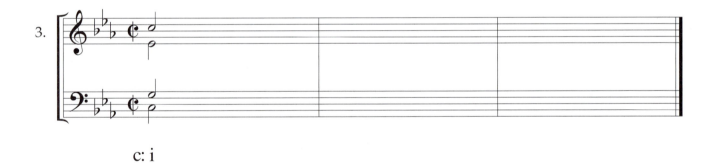

4.

D: I

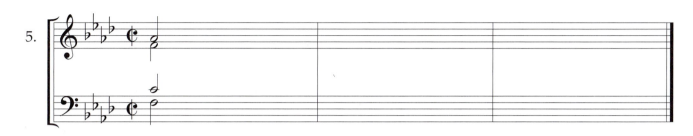

5.

f: i

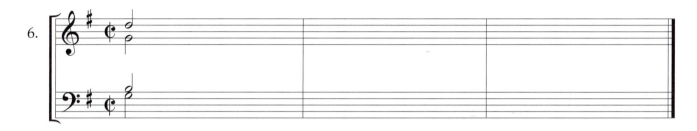

6.

G: I

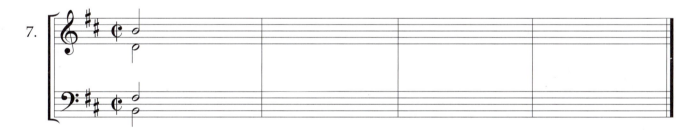

7.

b: i

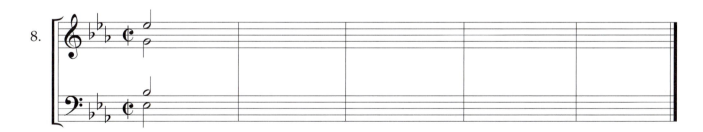

8.

E♭: I

9.

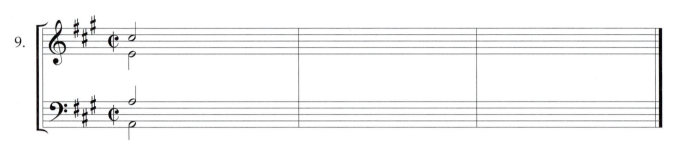

A: I

10.

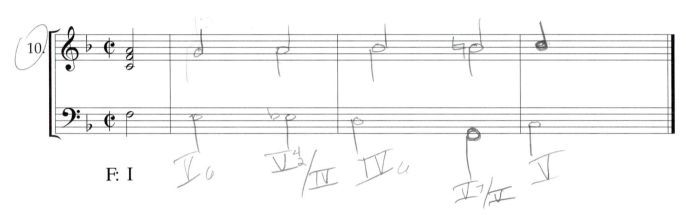

F: I   I₆   V⁴₂/IV   IV₆   V⁷/V   V

11.

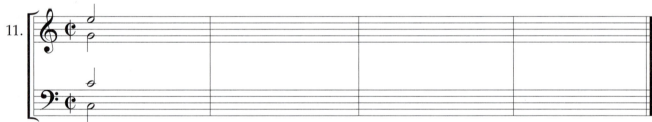

C: I

12.

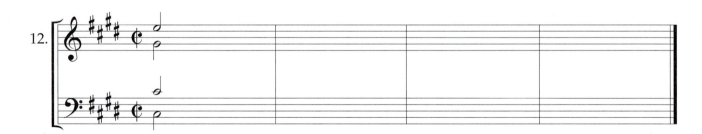

c#: i

Phrase-length Exercises

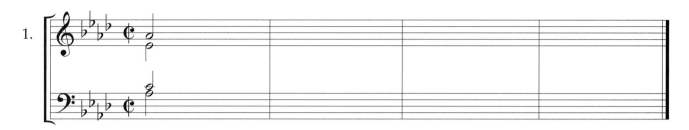

1.

Ab: I

2.

Bb: I

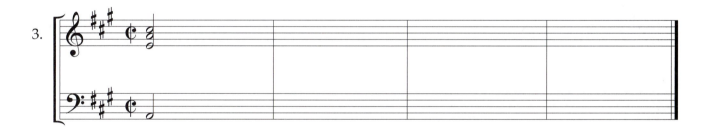

3.

A: I

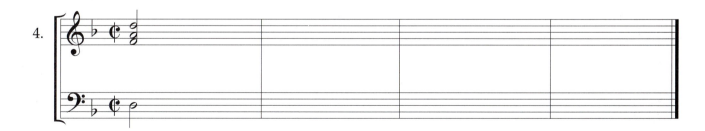

4.

d: i

5.

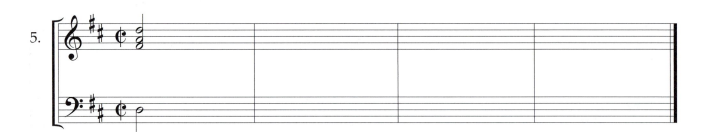

D: I

6.

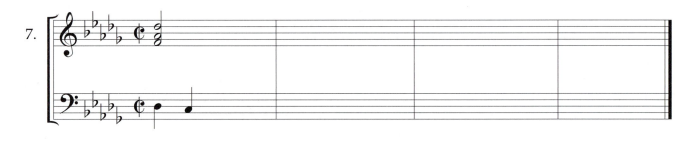

g: i

7.

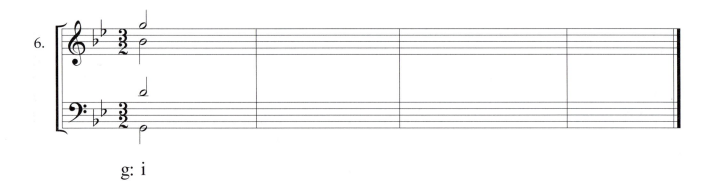

D♭: I

8.

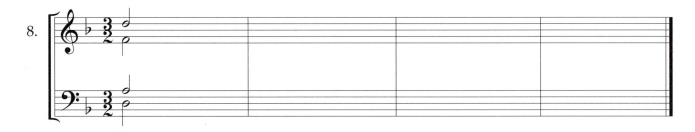

d: i

9.

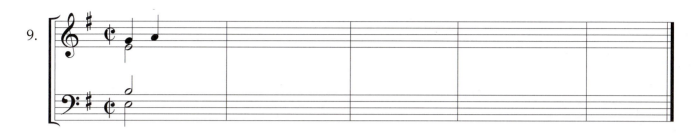

e: i

10.

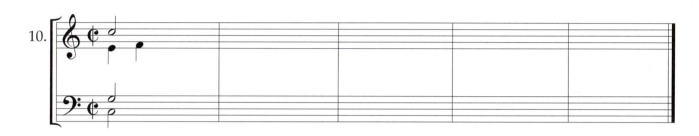

C: I

11.

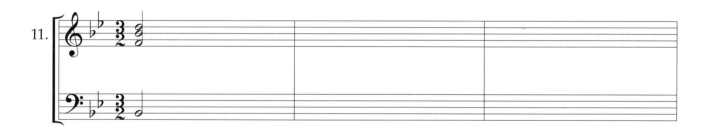

B♭: I

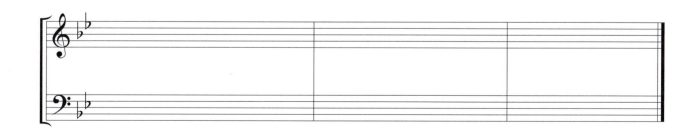

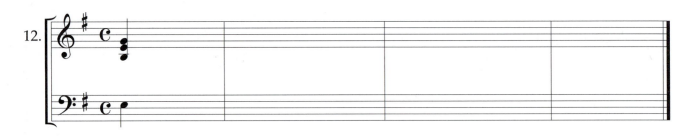

12.

e: i

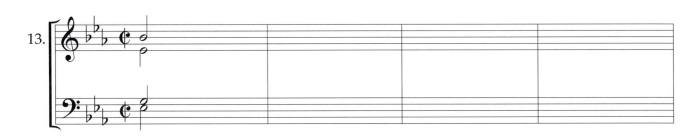

13.

E♭: I

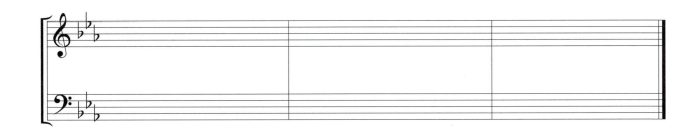

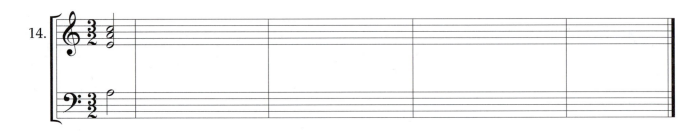

14.

a: i

Harmonic Dictation: QUIZ NO. 2

1.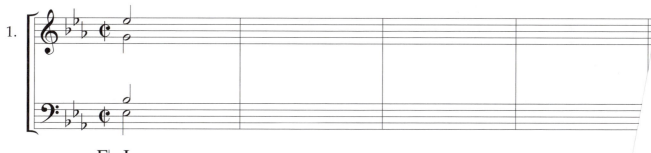

E♭: I

2.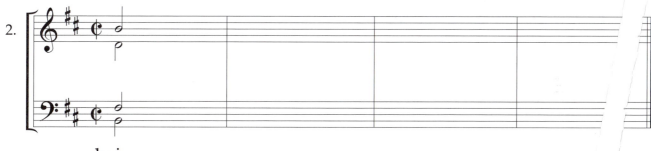

b: i

3.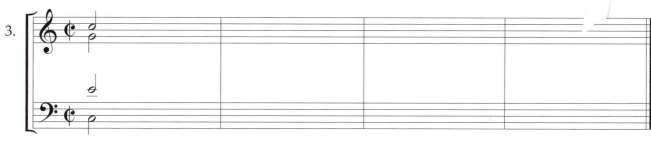

C: I

4.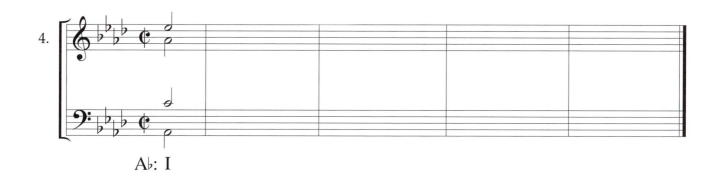

A♭: I

5.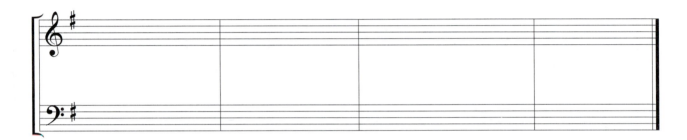

G: V V$_2^4$

Harmonic Dictation: QUIZ NO. 3

1.

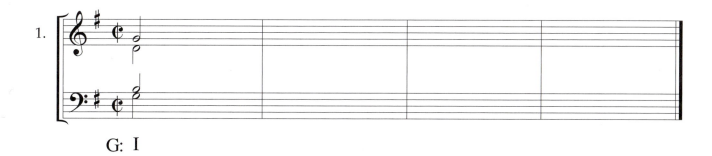

G: I

2.

D: V^7

3.

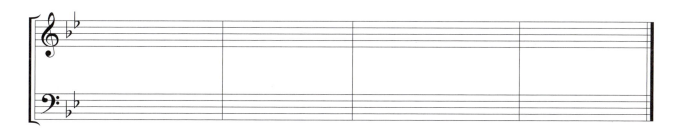

B♭: I

4.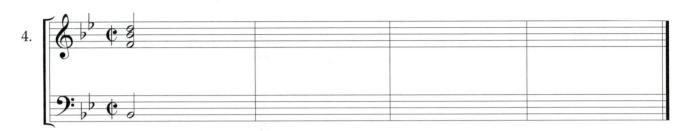

B♭: I

5.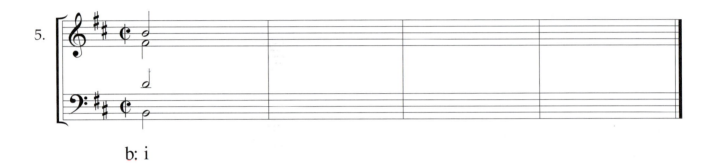

b: i

Unit 14

Examples from Music Literature

1. Johann Sebastian Bach. *Herr, wie du willst, so shick's mit mir* (chorale)

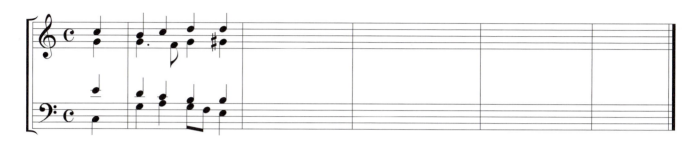

2. Johann Sebastian Bach. *Jesu, meiner Seelen Wonne* (chorale)

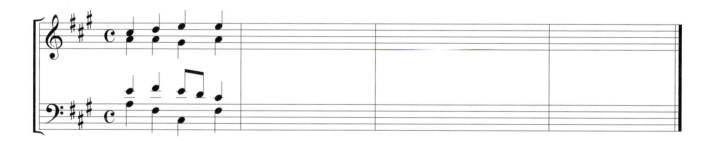

3. Johann Sebastian Bach. *Wer nur den lieben Gott lässt walten* (chorale)

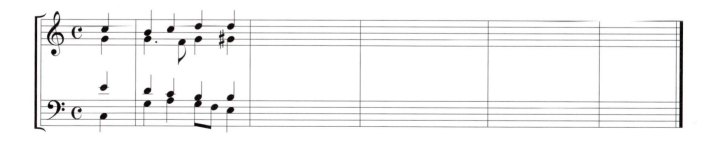

4. Johann Sebastian Bach. Minuet in G Minor

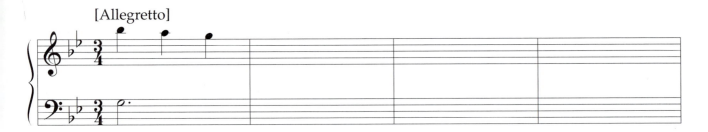

5. Edward MacDowell. *To a Wild Rose*, Op. 51, No. 1

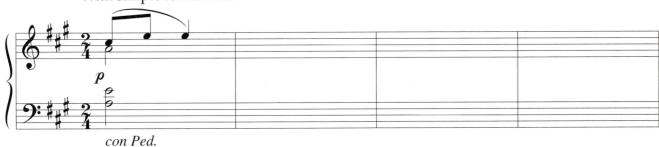

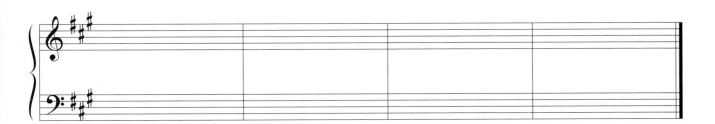

6. Carl Maria von Weber. German Dance

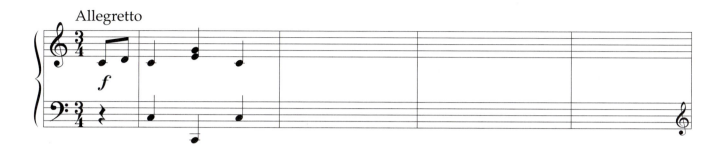

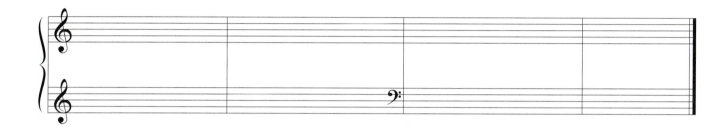

7. Frederic Chopin. Valse, Op. 69, No. 1

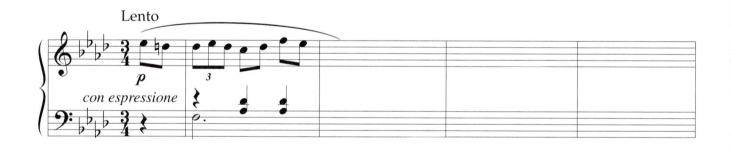

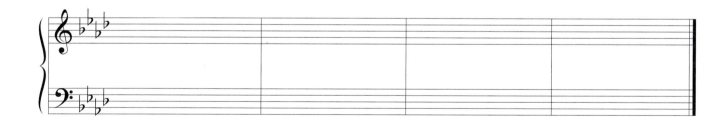

Class:

Professor:

Name: _____

8. Wolfgang Amadeus Mozart. String Quartet, K. 158, mvt. I

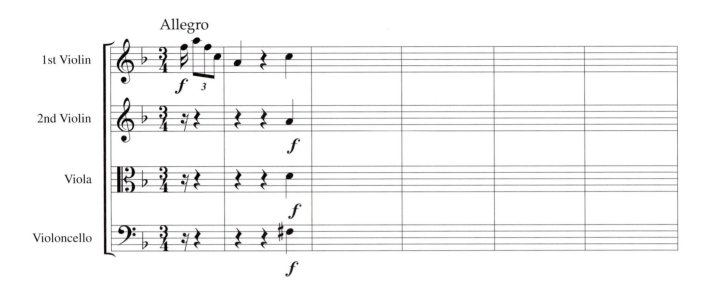

9. Joseph Haydn. Divertimento in D

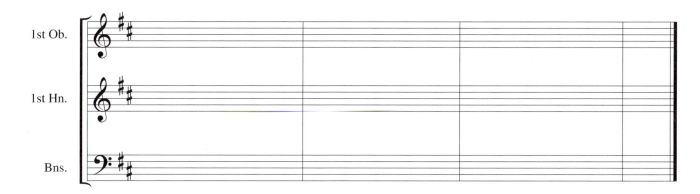

10. Ludwig van Beethoven. String Quartet, Op. 18, No. 6, mvt. I

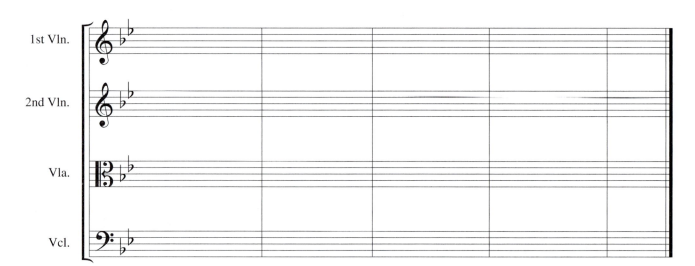

QUIZ NO. 1

1. Johann Sebastian Bach. *Jesu, meiner Seelen Wonne* (chorale)

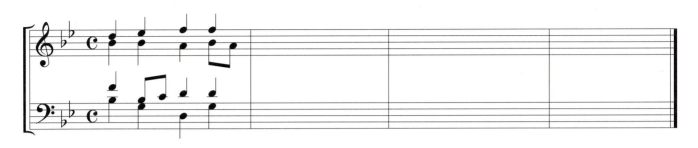

2. Johann Sebastian Bach. *Es woll' uns Gott genadig sein* (chorale)

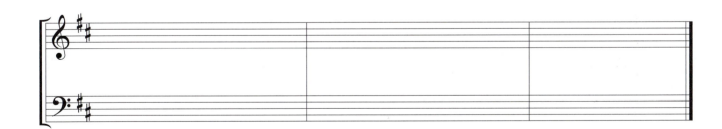

Name: _____

QUIZ NO. 2

1. Ludwig van Beethoven. *Romanze* from Sonatina in G

2. Frederic Chopin. Prelude, Op. 28, No. 7

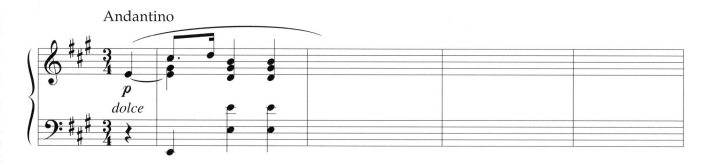

QUIZ NO. 3

Joseph Haydn. Divertimento in G, Hob. II:3

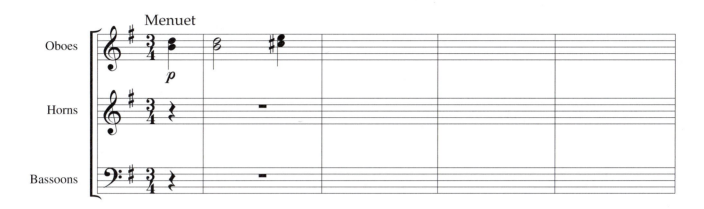

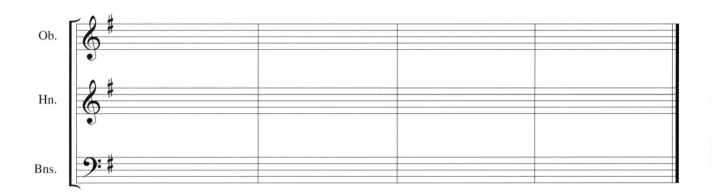

Unit 15

Melodic Dictation: Modulation to closely related keys

Melodies

1.
Moderato

2.
Andantino
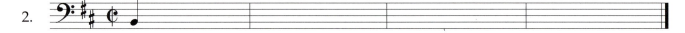

3.
Grazioso

4.
Allegretto

5.
Maestoso

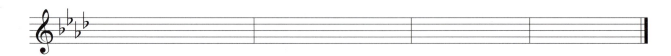

Largo

6.

Con spirito

7.

Calmo

8.

Allegro

9.

Ben marcato

10.

Allegretto

11.

Ritmico

12.

Cantabile

13.

14.

Allegro

15.

Moderato assai

16.

Andante

17.

Tempo di Minuet

18.

Comodo 𝄋

Fine

D.S. al Fine

Melodic Dictation: QUIZ NO. 1

1.

2.

3.

4.

5.

Melodic Dictation: QUIZ NO. 2

Doloroso

1.

Allegro

2.

Cantabile

3.

Animato

4.

Comodo

5.

Melodic Dictation: QUIZ NO. 3

Con moto

1.

Andantino

2.

Allegretto

3.

Andante

4.

Presto

5.

Harmonic Dictation: Modulation to closely related keys

Phrase-length Exercises

1.
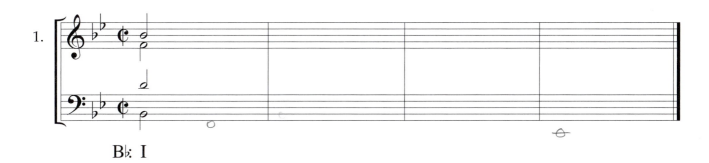

Bb: I

2.
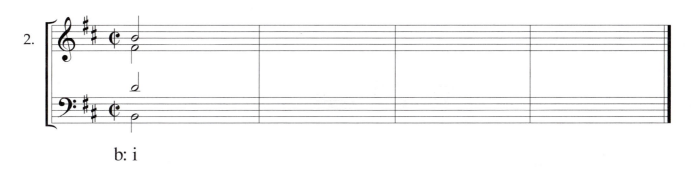

b: i

3.
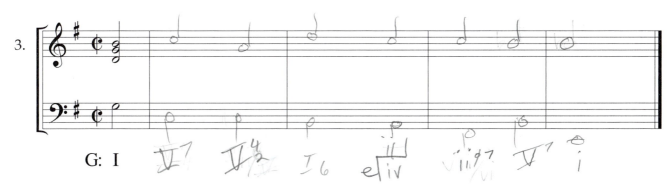

G: I Ⅴ⁷ Ⅴ⁴₂ I₆ e: iv viiø⁷/Ⅵ Ⅴ⁷ i

4.
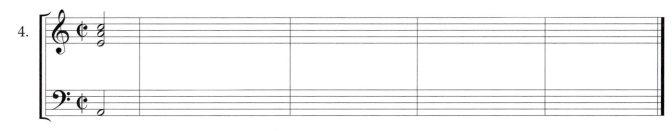

a: i

5.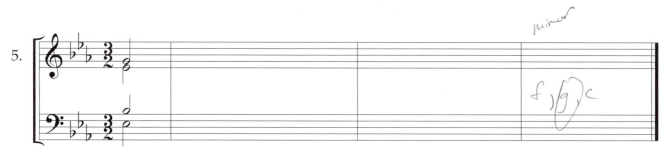

Eb: I

6.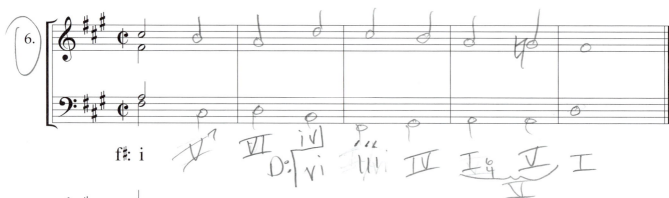

f#: i

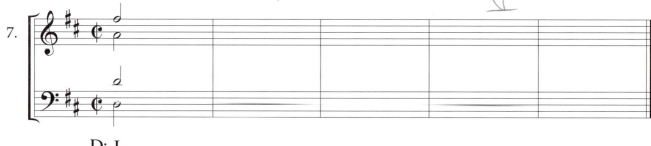

7.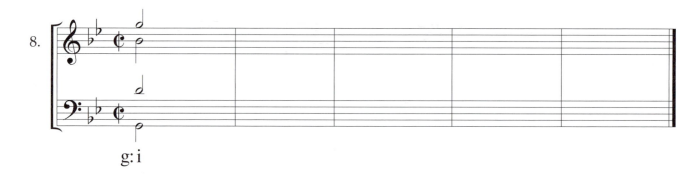

D: I

8.

g: i

Class:

Professor:

Name: _____

9.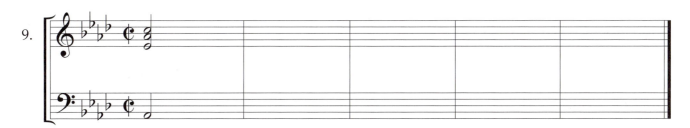

Ab: I

10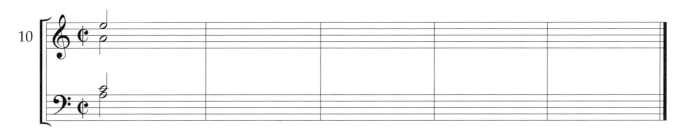

a: i

11.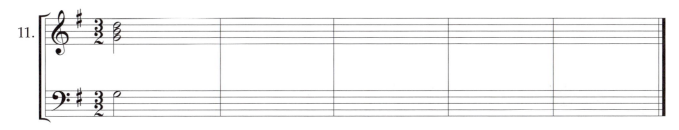

G: I

12.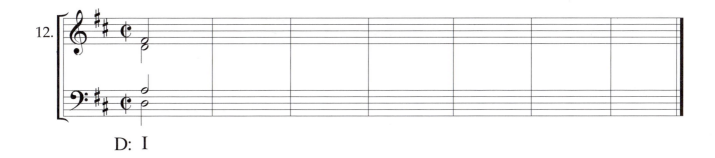

D: I

13.

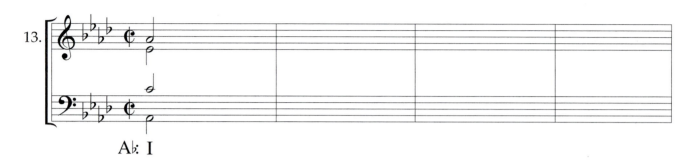

Ab: I

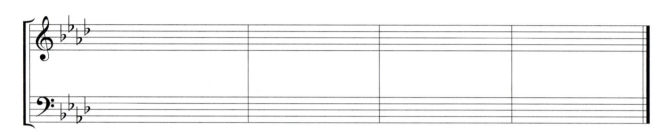

14.

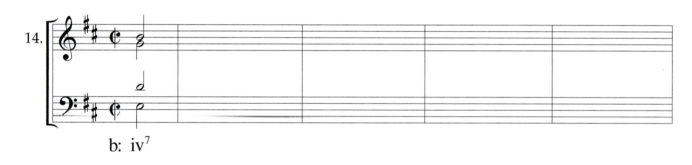

b: iv⁷

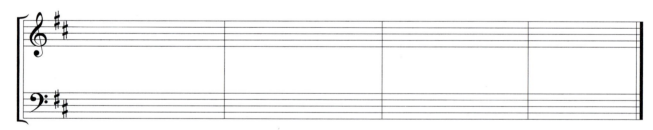

5.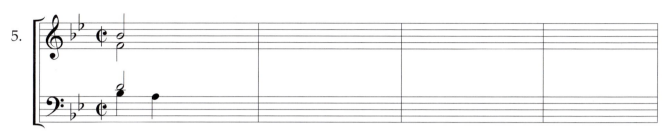

B♭: I

Harmonic Dictation: QUIZ NO. 2

1.
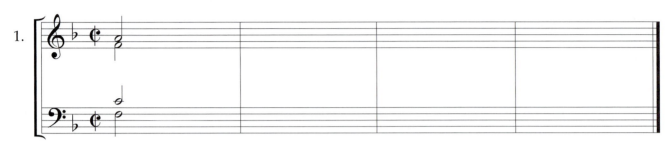

F: I

2.

b: i

3.
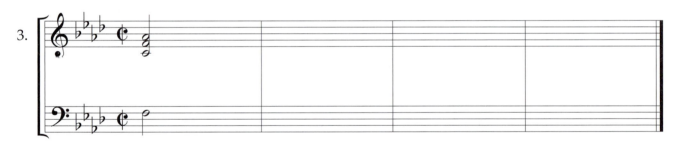

f: i

4.
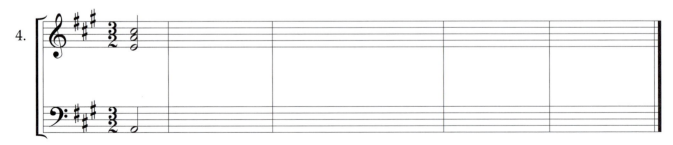

A: I

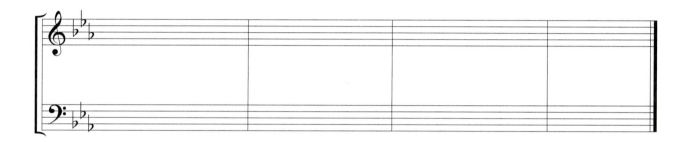

5.

E♭: I

Class: _____   Name: _____

Professor: _____

Harmonic Dictation: QUIZ NO. 3

1.
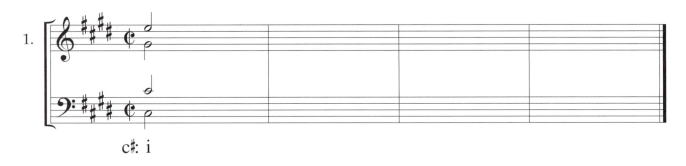

c#: i

2.
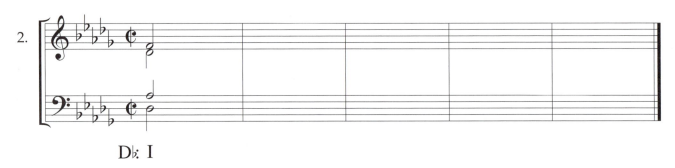

D♭: I

3.
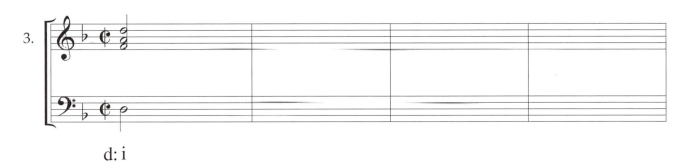

d: i

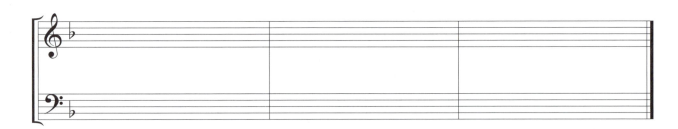

4.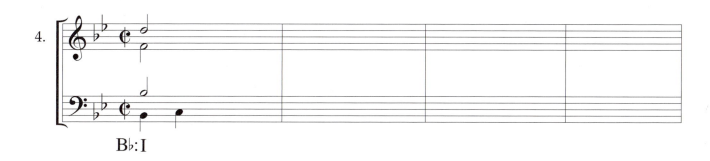

Bb: I

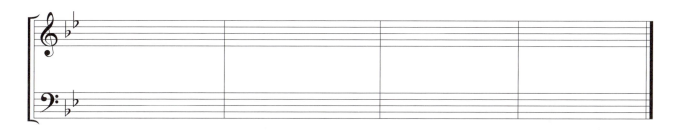

5.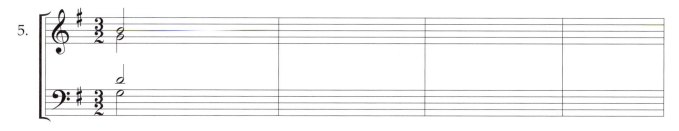

G: I

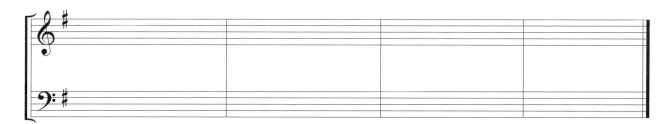

Unit 16

Rhythmic Dictation: Quintuple meter

Preliminary Exercises

1.

2.

3.

4.

5.

6.

Comprehensive Exercises

7.

8.

9.

10.

11.

12.

13.

14.

15.

16.

17.

18.

Rhythmic Dictation: QUIZ NO. 1

1.

2.

3.

4.

5.

Rhythmic Dictation: QUIZ NO. 2

1.

2.

3.

4.

5.

Rhythmic Dictation: QUIZ NO. 3

1.

2.

3.

4.

5.

Melodic Dictation: The Neapolitan sixth chord, augmented sixth chords, and modulation to distantly related keys

Preliminary Exercises

1.

2.

3.

4.

5.

6.

7.

8.

Melodies

Andante

1.

Andantino

2.

Doloroso

3.

Marziale

4.

Moderato

5.

Andantino

6.

Allegro marcato

7.

Allegretto

8.

Larghetto

9.

Giocoso

10.

Moderato

11.

Moderato

12.

Con passione

5.

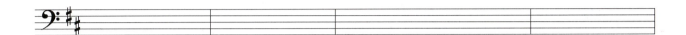

Melodic Dictation: QUIZ NO. 2

Andantino

1.

Larghetto

2.

Allegro

3.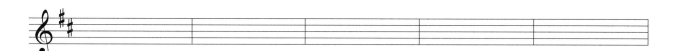

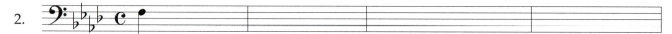

Andante

4.

Andantino

5.

Melodic Dictation: QUIZ NO. 3

1.

2.

3.

Capriccioso

4.

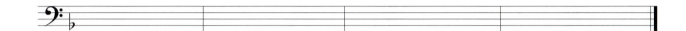

Comodo

5.

Class: _____   Name: _____

Professor:

Harmonic Dictation: The Neapolitan sixth chord, augmented sixth chords, enharmonic modulation

Basic Progressions

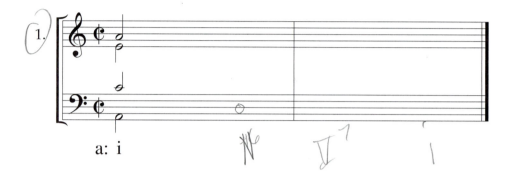

1. a: i

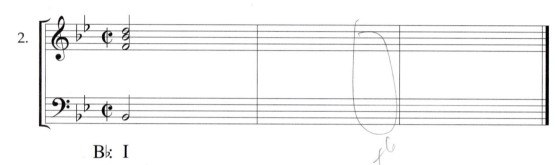

2. B♭: I

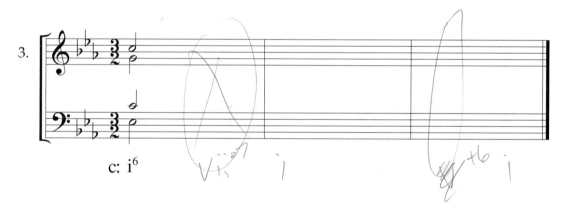

3. c: i⁶

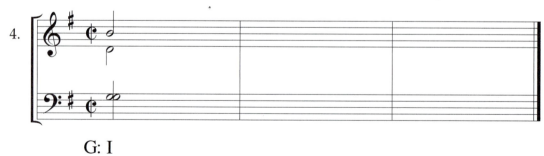

4. G: I

5.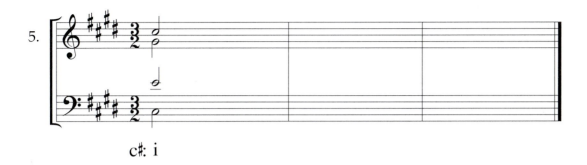

c#: i

6.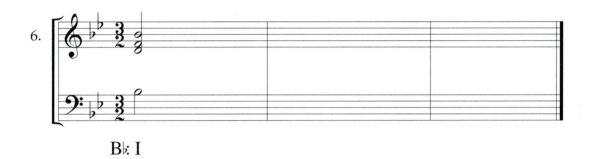

Bb: I

7.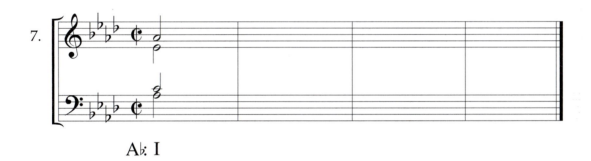

Ab: I

8.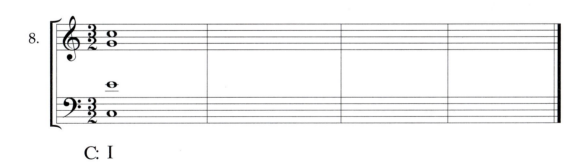

C: I

9.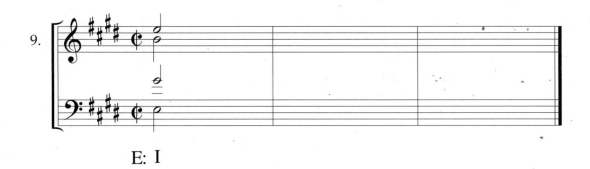

    E: I

10.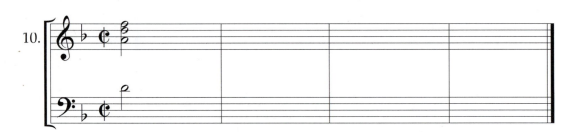

    d: i

Name: _____

Phrase-length Exercises

5.

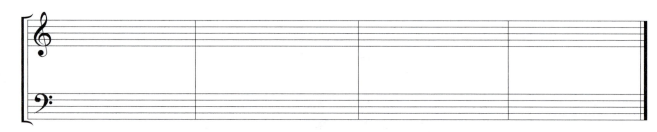

C: I

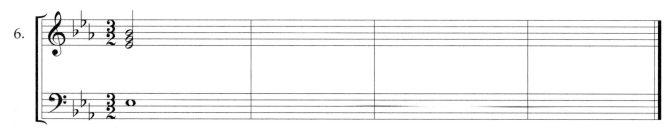

6.

E♭: I

7.

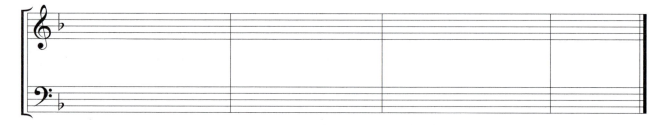

F: I

8.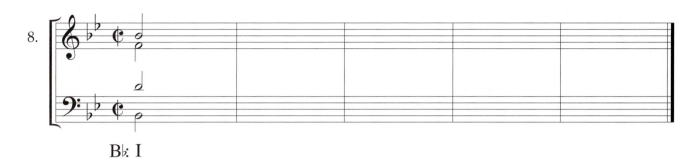

Bb: I

9.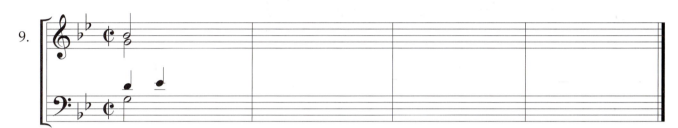

g: i

10.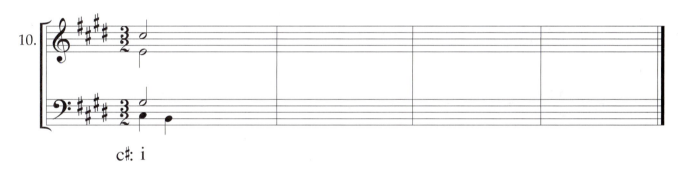

c#: i

11.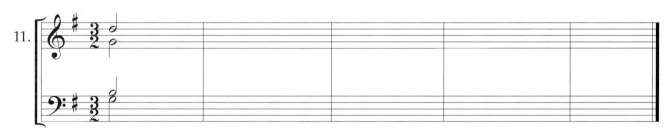

G: I

12.

Ab: I

13.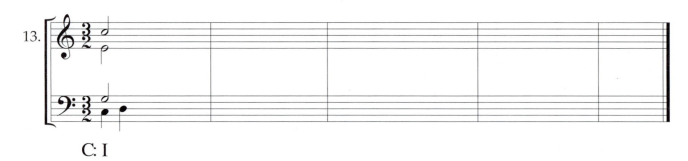

C: I

14.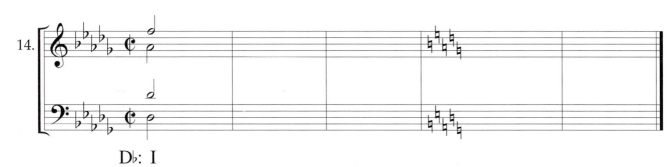

D♭: I

15.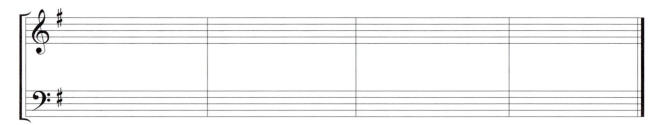

G: I

Harmonic Dictation: QUIZ NO. 1

1.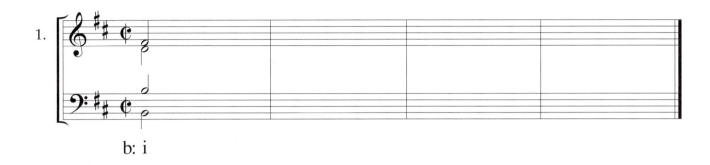

    b: i

2.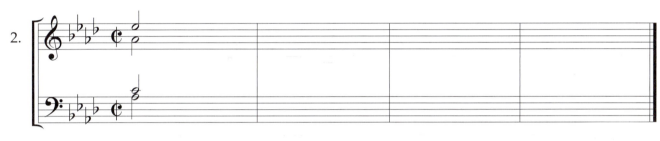

    A♭: I

3.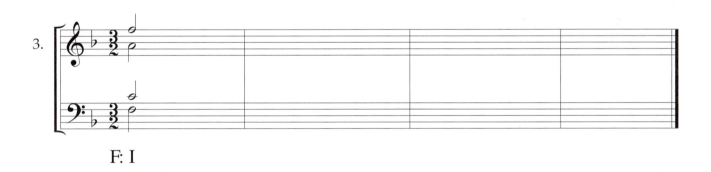

    F: I

4.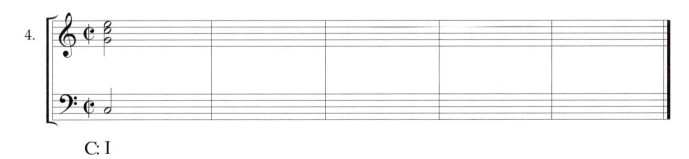

    C: I

5.

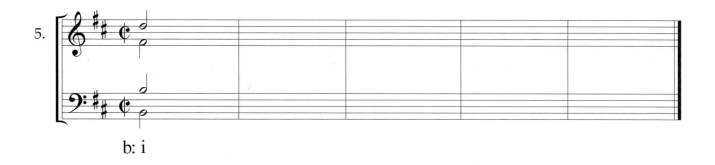

b: i

Name: _____

Unit 17 ═══════════════════════════════════════

Examples from Music Literature

1. Johann Sebastian Bach. *Ach Gott, von Himmel sieh' darein* (chorale)

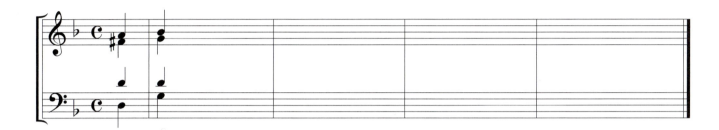

2. Johann Sebastian Bach. *Befiehl du deine Wege* (chorale)

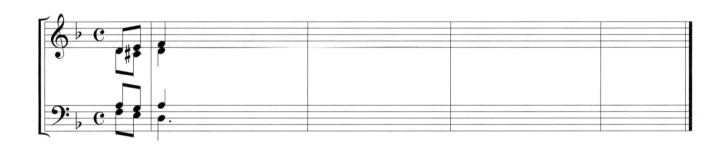

3. Johann Sebastian Bach. *Ach Gott, wie manches Herzeleid* (chorale)

4. Johann Sebastian Bach. *Hilf, Herr Jesu, lass gelingen* (chorale)

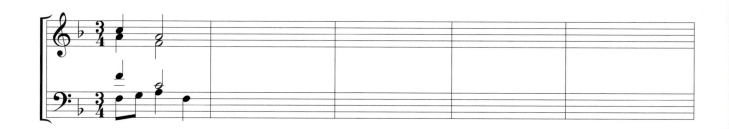

5. Johann Sebastian Bach. Bourrée, French Overture

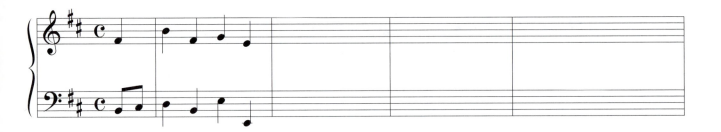

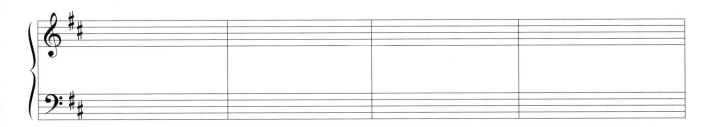

6. Jeremiah Clarke. Jigg

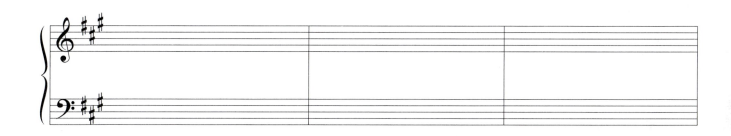

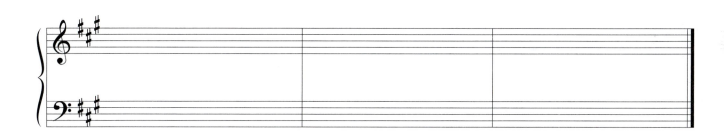

7. Antonio Diabelli. Rondino

Allegretto

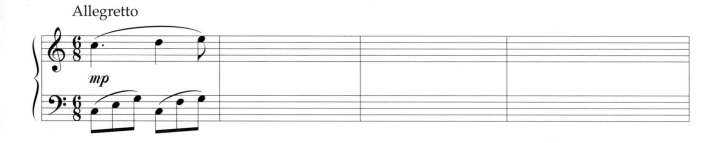

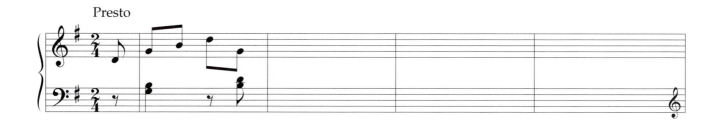

8. Joseph Haydn. Sonata, Hob. XVI:27, mvt. III

Presto

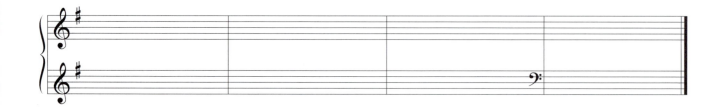

9. Ludwig van Beethoven. Bagatelle, Op. 119, No. 1

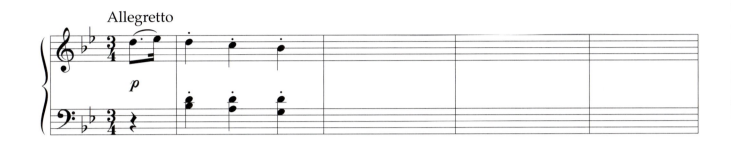

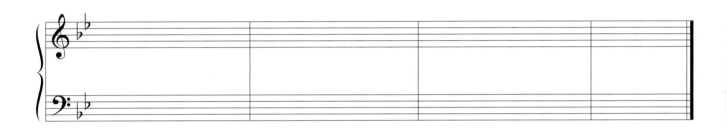

10. Ludwig van Beethoven. Minuet in G Major, WoO 10, No. 2

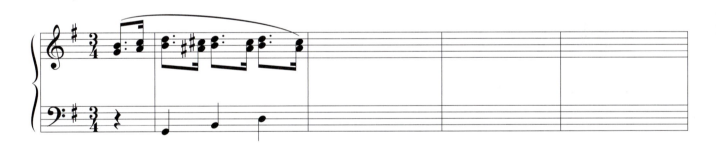

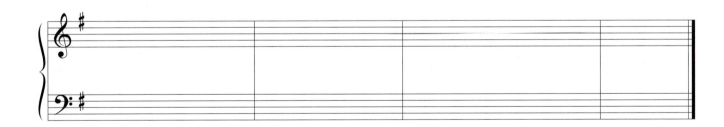

11. Mikail Ivanovich Glinka. Waltz, Op. 39, No. 15

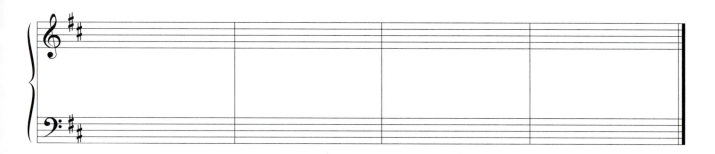

12. Franz Schubert. Scherzo in B-flat

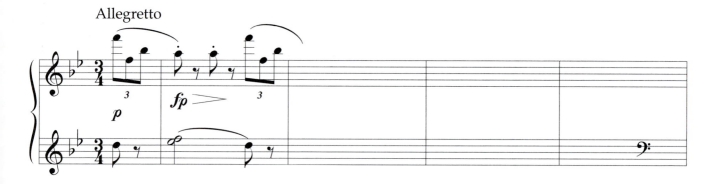

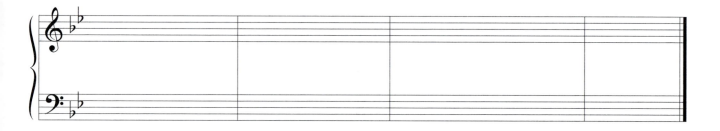

13. Joseph Haydn. Divertimento, Hob. II:18, mvt. III, Trio

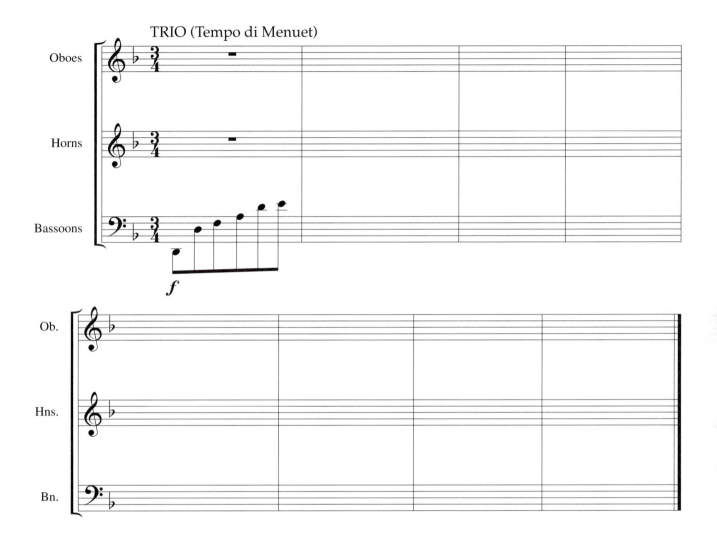

14. Ludwig van Beethoven. Quartet, Op. 18, No. 1, mvt. III

Allegro molto

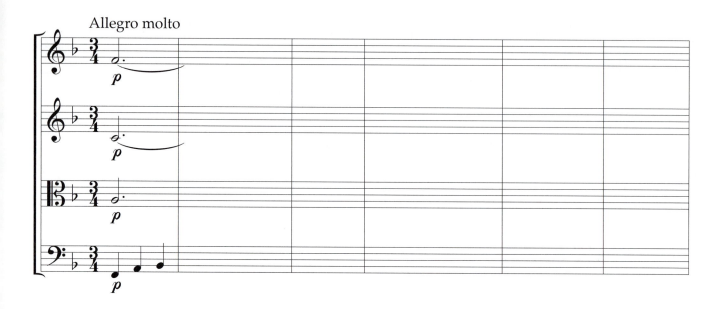

15. Ludwig van Beethoven. Quartet, Op. 18, No. 4, mvt. III

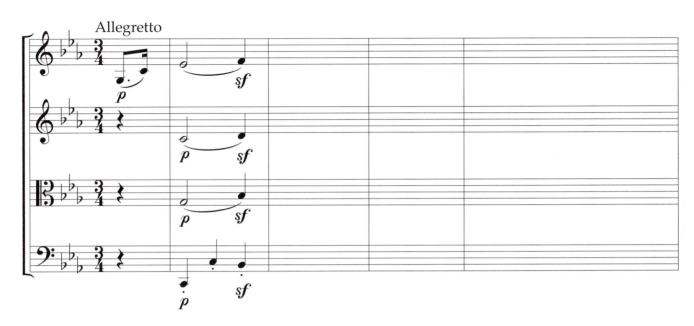

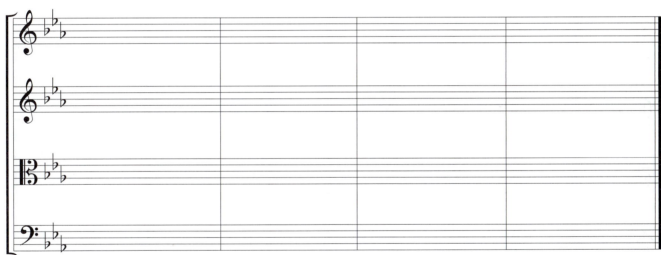

16. Ludwig van Beethoven. Quartet, Op. 18, No. 4, mvt. IV

17. Wolfgang Amadeus Mozart. Quartet, K. 421, mvt. III

MENUETTO (Allegretto)

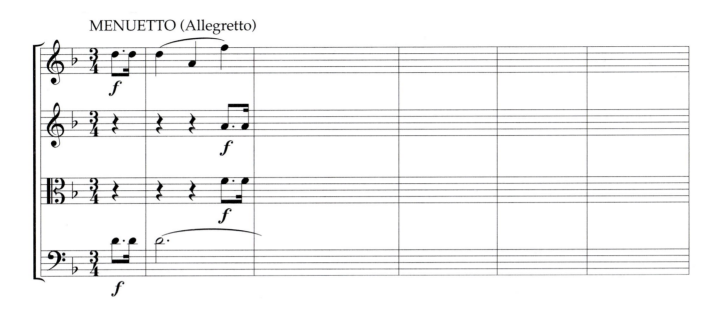

18. Wolfgang Amadeus Mozart. Quartet, K. 170, mvt. I

Andante

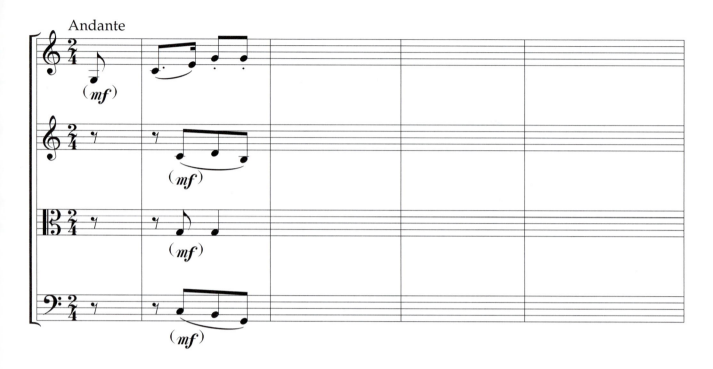

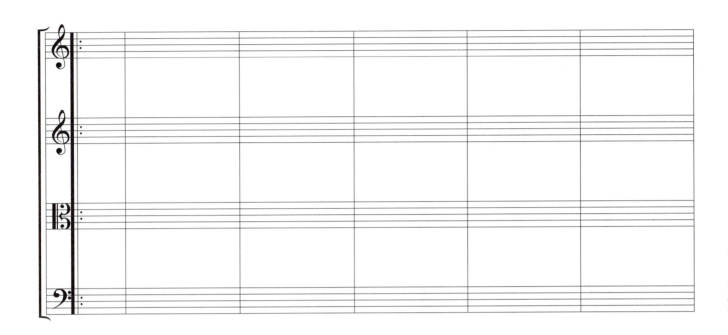

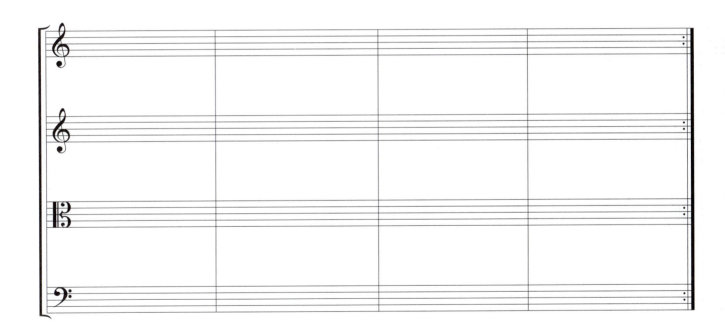

QUIZ NO. 1

1. Johann Sebastian Bach. *Befiehl du deine Wege* (chorale)

2. Domenico Scarlatti. Sonata, Longo 83

3. Joseph Haydn. Sonata, Hob. XVI:37, mvt. III

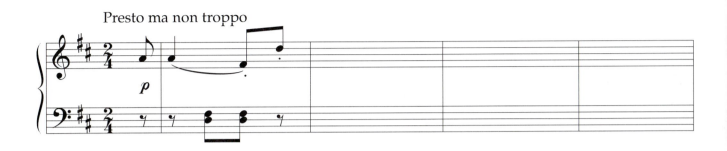

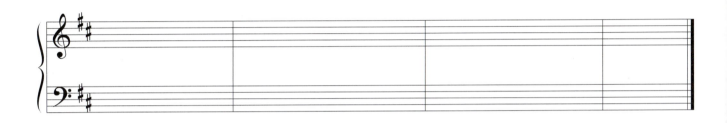

4. Ludwig van Beethoven. Sonata "Pathetique," Op. 13, mvt. III

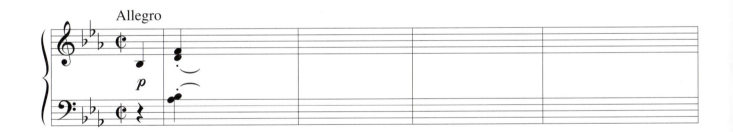

QUIZ NO. 2

1. Johann Sebastian Bach. *Meine Seel' erhebt den Herren* (chorale)

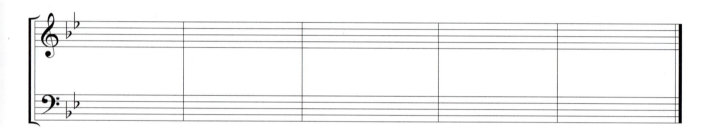

2. Ludwig van Beethoven. Sonata, Op. 14, No. 1, mvt. II

Maggiore Allegretto

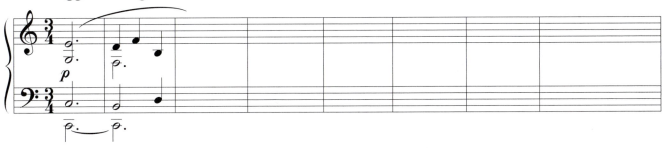

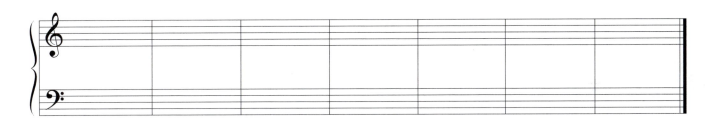

3. Johannes Brahms. Waltz, Op. 39, No. 15

Tempo giusto

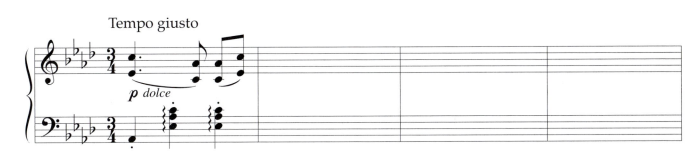

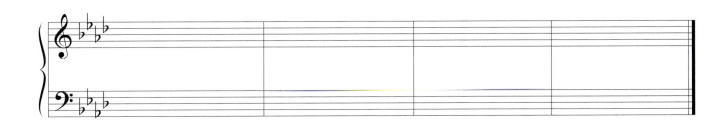

4. Ludwig van Beethoven. Quartet, Op. 18, No. 2, mvt. III, Trio

TRIO   Allegro

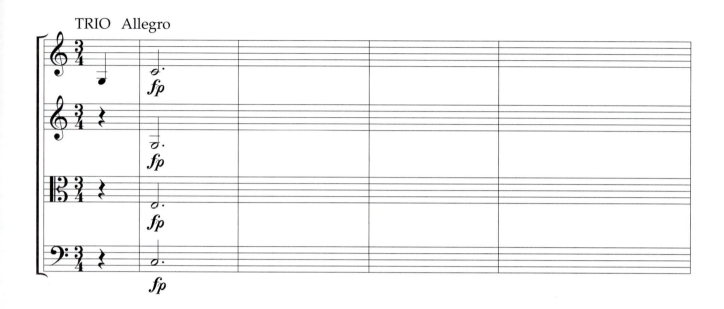

QUIZ NO. 3

1. Johann Sebastian Bach. *Jesu, meine Freude* (chorale)

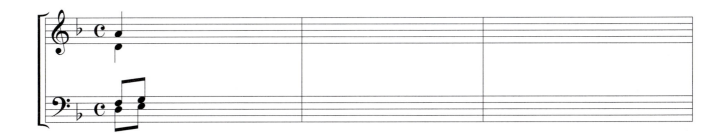

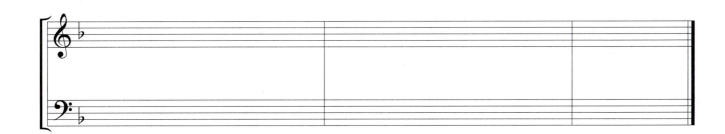

2. Robert Schumann. "Important Event," *Scenes from Childhood*, Op. 15, No. 6

3. Edvard Grieg. Rigaudon, Op. 40, No. 5, Trio

Allegro con brio un poco meno mosso

4. Ludwig van Beethoven. Quartet, Op. 18, No. 3, mvt. III

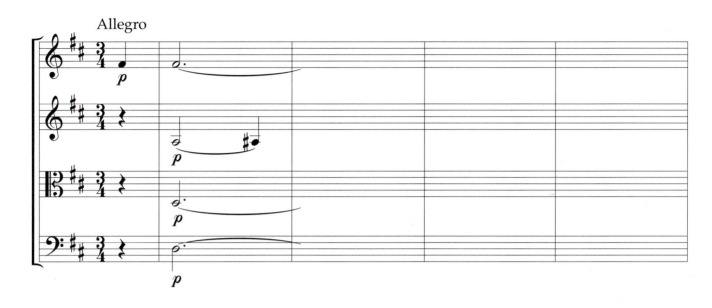

Unit 18

Rhythmic Dictation: Irregular meters

1.

2.

3.

4.

5.

6.

7.

8.

9.

10.

11.

12.

13.

14.

Rhythmic Dictation: QUIZ NO. 1

1.

2.

3.

4.

5.

Rhythmic Dictation: QUIZ NO. 2

1.

2.

3.

4.

5.

Melodic Dictation: Diatonic modes

Moderato bucolico

1.

Misterioso

2.

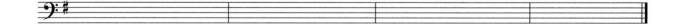

Tempo di valse

3.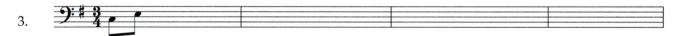

Andante

4.

5.
Con forza

6.
Cantabile

7.
Vigoroso

8.
Contempletivo

9.

Allegretto

10.

Grazioso

11.

Ruhig

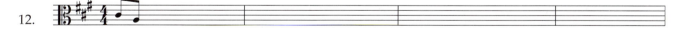

12.

Scherzando

13.

Energico

14.

Andantino

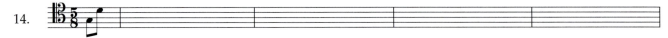

Melodic Dictation: QUIZ NO. 1

Moderato

1.

Marcato

2.

Doloroso

3.

Ritmico

4.

Amabile

5.

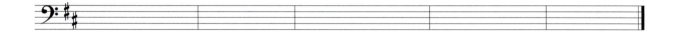

Class: _____   Name: _____

Professor: _____

Melodic Dictation: QUIZ NO. 2

Gracieuse

1.

Vigoroso

2.

Andantino

3.

Allegretto

4.

Simply

5.

Harmonic Dictation: Diatonic modes

1.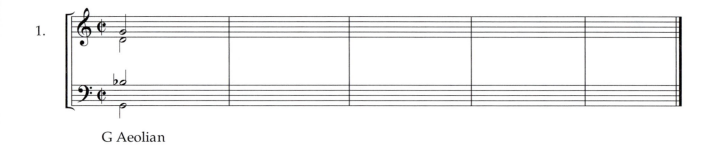

G Aeolian

2.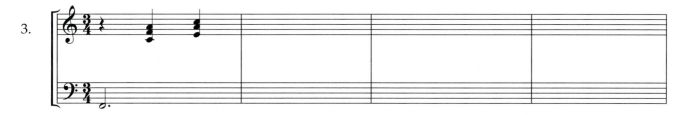

B Phrygian

3.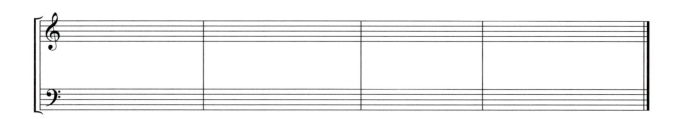

F Lydian

4.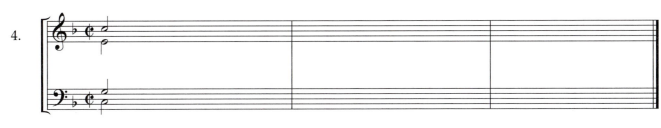

C Mixolydian

5.

A Dorian

6.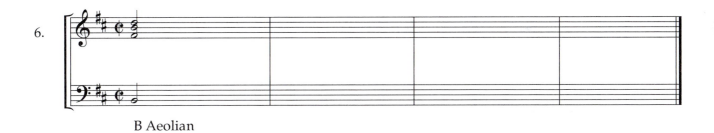

B Aeolian

7.

D Phrygian

8.

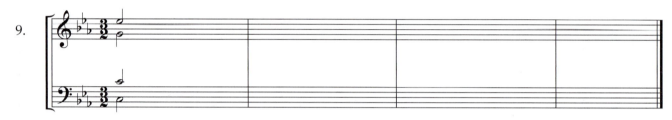

Eb Lydian

9.

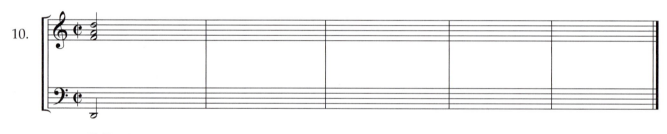

C Aeolian

10.

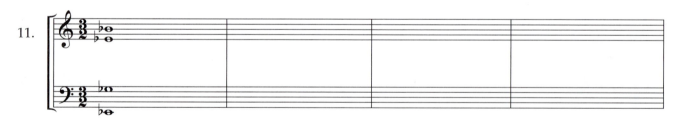

D Dorian

11.

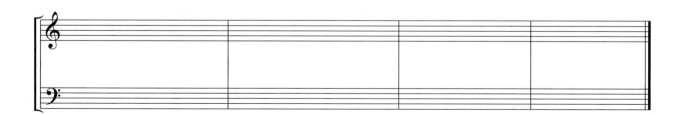

Eb Aeolian

12.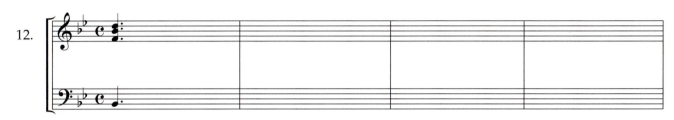

Bb Mixolydian

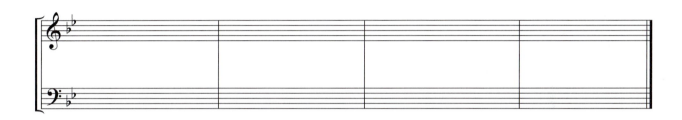

13.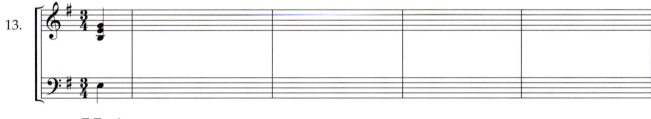

E Dorian

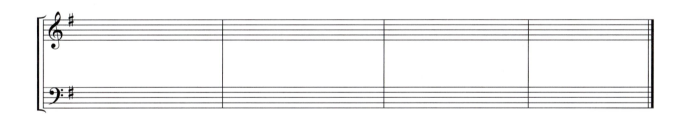

14.

C Phrygian

Harmonic Dictation: QUIZ NO. 1

1.
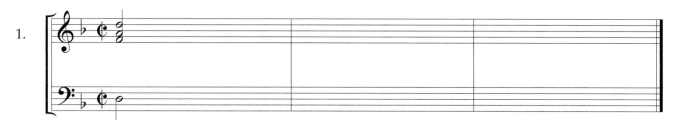

D Aeolian

2.
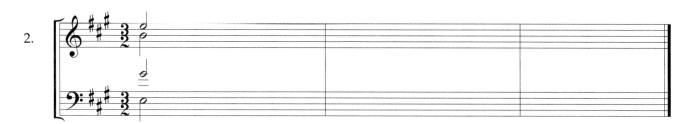

E Mixolydian

3.
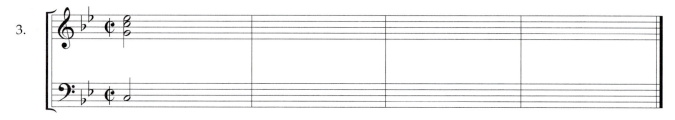

C Dorian

4.
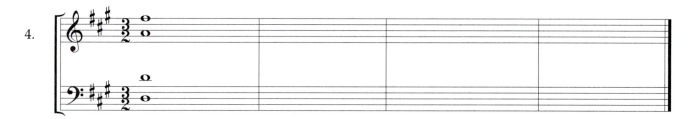

D Lydian

5.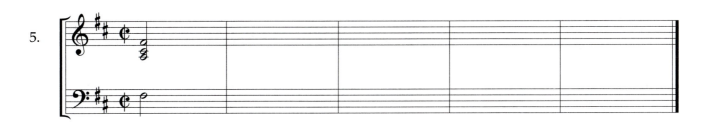

F# Phrygian

Harmonic Dictation: QUIZ NO. 2

1.

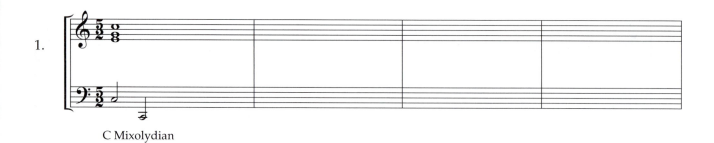

C Mixolydian

2.

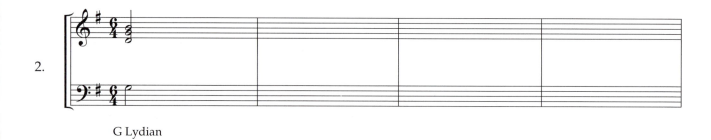

G Lydian

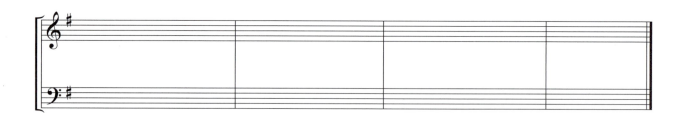

3.

A Dorian

4.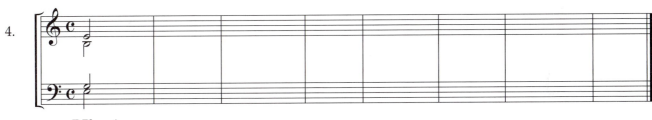

E Phrygian

5.

G Aeolian

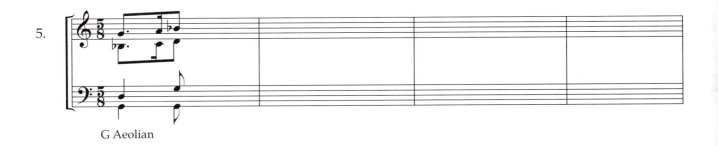

Unit 19

Rhythmic Dictation: Changing meters

1.

2.

3.

4.

5.

6.

7. $\frac{7}{8}$ ♩. ——————— $\frac{3}{4}$ ——————— $\frac{5}{8}$ ——————— $\frac{3}{4}$ ——————— $\frac{7}{8}$ ———————

——————— $\frac{3}{4}$ ——————— $\frac{7}{8}$ ——————— $\frac{3}{4}$ ———————

8. $\frac{3}{8}$ ♩♪♪ $\frac{3}{4}$ ——————— $\frac{3}{8}$ ——————— $\frac{2}{4}$ ——————— $\frac{3}{8}$ ——————— $\frac{3}{4}$ ———————

9. $\frac{3}{4}$ ♩. ——————— $\frac{2}{4}$ ——————— $\frac{3}{4}$ ——————— $\frac{2}{4}$ ——————— $\frac{3}{4}$ ———————

——————— $\frac{2}{4}$ ——————— $\frac{3}{4}$ ——————— $\frac{2}{4}$ ———————

10. $\frac{6}{8}$ ♩.♪ $\frac{4}{8}$ ——————— $\frac{3}{8}$ ——————— $\frac{2}{4}$ ——————— $\frac{3}{8}$ ——————— $\frac{3}{4}$ ———————

$\frac{3}{8}$ ——————— $\frac{4}{8}$ ——————— $\frac{6}{8}$ ——————— $\frac{4}{8}$ ——————— $\frac{5}{8}$ ——————— $\frac{4}{8}$ ———————

11. $\frac{2}{4}$ ♩ ——————— $\frac{3}{4}$ ——————— $\frac{5}{8}$ ——————— $\frac{2}{4}$ ——————— $\frac{3}{8}$ ———————

$\frac{2}{4}$ ——————— $\frac{5}{8}$ ——————— $\frac{2}{4}$ ——————— $\frac{7}{8}$ ——————— $\frac{3}{4}$ ———————

12. $\frac{6}{8}$ ♪♪♪ $\frac{3}{4}$ ——————— $\frac{5}{8}$ ——————— $\frac{3}{4}$ ——————— $\frac{2}{4}$ ———————

$\frac{5}{8}$ ——————— $\frac{3}{4}$ ——————— $\frac{6}{8}$ ——————— $\frac{2}{4}$ ——————— $\frac{3}{4}$ ———————

13.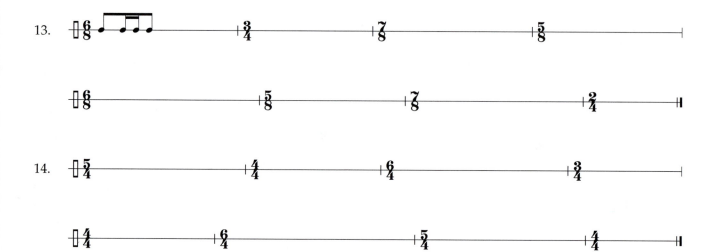

14.

Class:

Professor:

Name: ______________________________

Rhythmic Dictation: QUIZ NO. 1

1.

2.

3.

4.

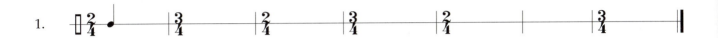

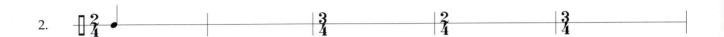

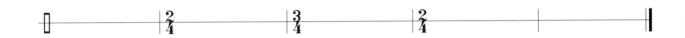

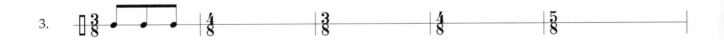

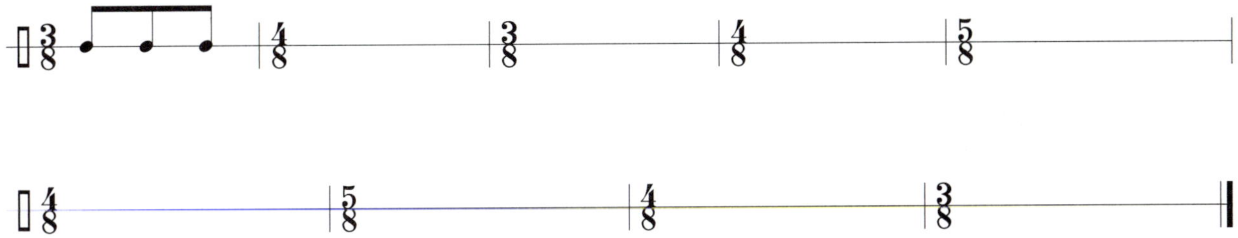

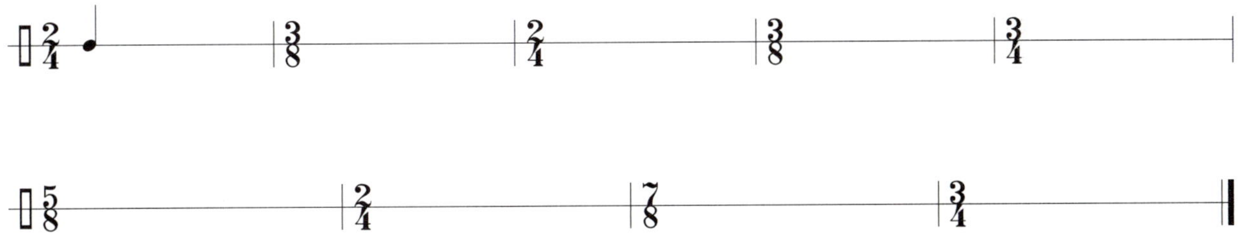

5.

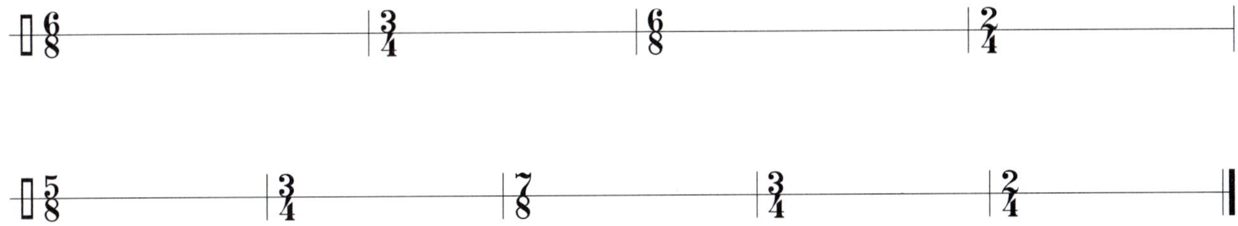

Rhythmic Dictation: QUIZ NO. 2

1.

2.

3.

4.

5.

Part Music Dictation: Pandiatonicism

Amabile

1.

Semplice

2.

Lent et grave

3.

Comodo

4.

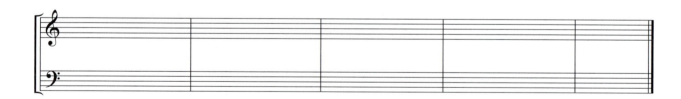

Modéré

5.

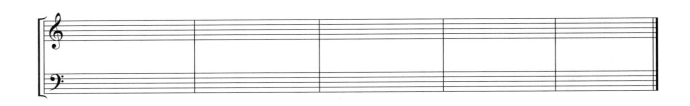

Grazioso

6.

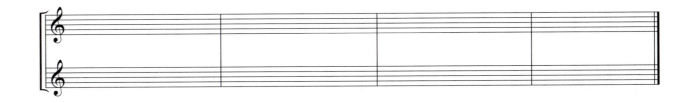

Andantino

7.

Allegro

8.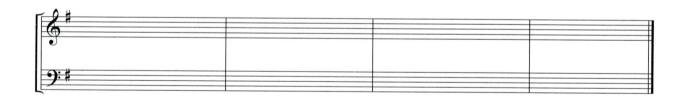

9.

10.

Andantino

11.

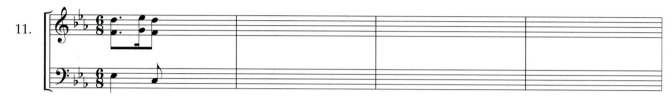

Allegro moderato

12.

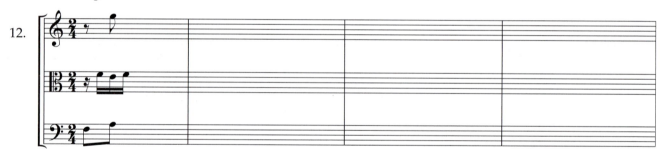

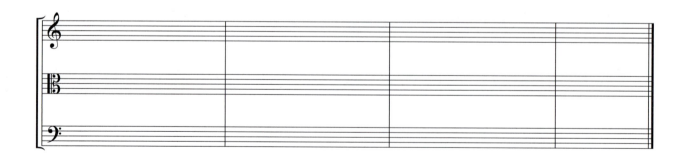

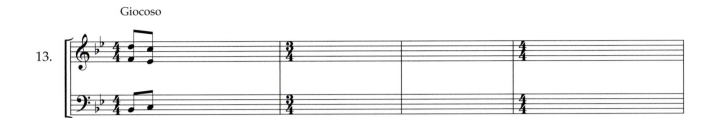

13.

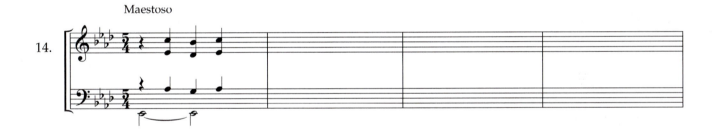

14.

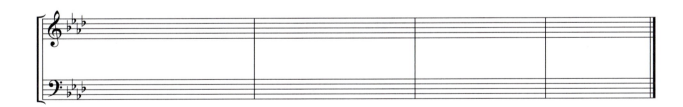

15.

Stately

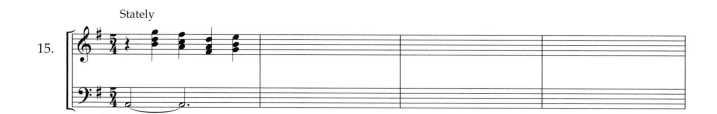

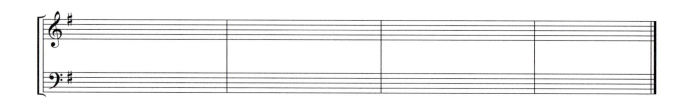

16.

Brillante

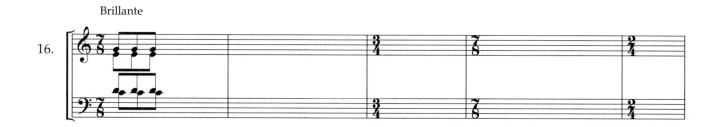

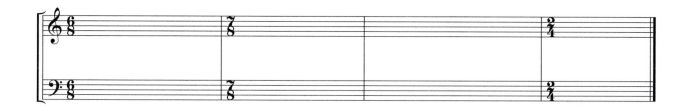

Part Music Dictation: QUIZ NO. 1

Piacevole

1.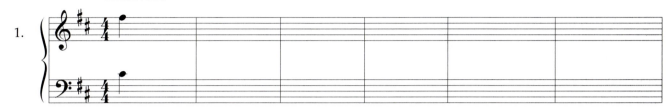

Andante

2.

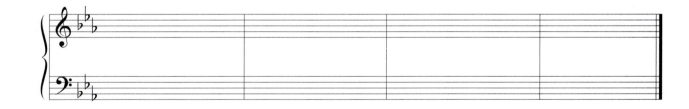

Giocoso

3.

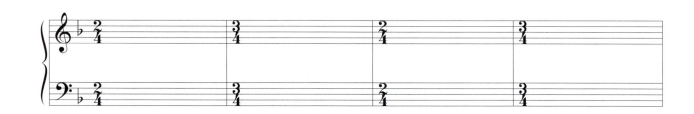

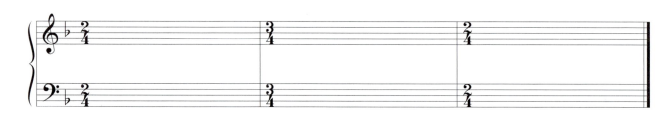

Sostenuto

4.

Fliessend

5.

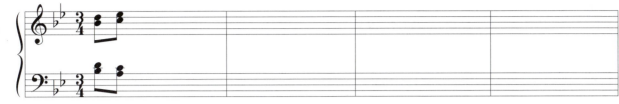

Part Music Dictation: QUIZ NO. 2

Tempo di Valse

1.
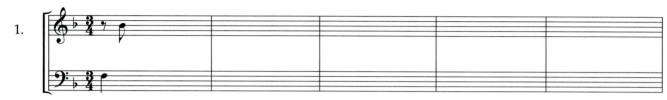

Allegretto

2.
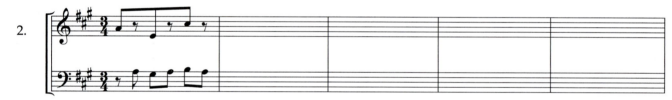

3.

Berceuse

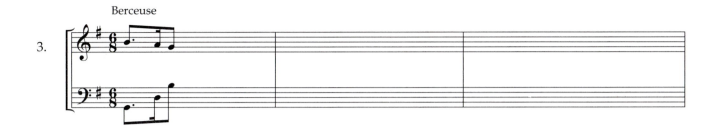

4.

Moderato

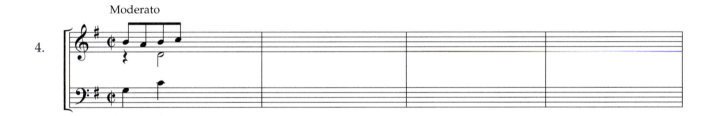

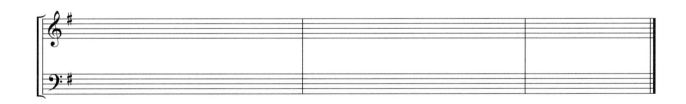

5.

Moderato

Unit 20

Rhythmic Dictation: Syncopation, including irregular and mixed meters

1.

2.

3.

4.

5.

6.

7.

8.

9.

10.

11.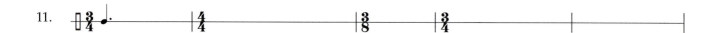

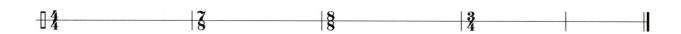

12.

13.

14.

Rhythmic Dictation: QUIZ NO. 1

1. $\frac{4}{4}$

2. $\frac{5}{4}$

3. $\frac{6}{8}$

4. $\frac{3}{4}$ ... $\frac{2}{4}$

   $\frac{3}{4}$ ... $\frac{7}{8}$ ... $\frac{3}{4}$ ... $\frac{2}{4}$ ... $\frac{3}{4}$

5. $\frac{2}{4}$ ... $\frac{3}{4}$ ... $\frac{5}{8}$ ... $\frac{3}{4}$ ... $\frac{3}{8}$

   $\frac{3}{4}$ ... $\frac{5}{8}$ ... $\frac{4}{4}$ ... $\frac{3}{8}$ ... $\frac{2}{4}$

Rhythmic Dictation: QUIZ NO. 2

1.

2.

3.

4. $\frac{5}{8}$ | $\frac{7}{8}$ | |

$\frac{6}{8}$ | $\frac{5}{8}$ | $\frac{6}{8}$ | $\frac{5}{8}$ |

$\frac{8}{8}$ | $\frac{7}{8}$ | $\frac{4}{8}$ ||

5. $\frac{5}{4}$ | $\frac{3}{4}$ | $\frac{4}{4}$ |

$\frac{5}{4}$ | $\frac{3}{4}$ | $\frac{5}{4}$ | $\frac{3}{4}$ | ||

Melodic Dictation: Extended and altered tertian harmony

1. Giocoso

2. Andante

3. Moderato

4. Allegro brillante

Moderato

5.

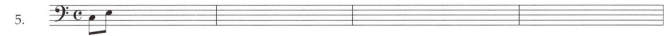

Grazioso

6.

Con moto

7.

Allegro ma non troppo

8.

9.

Andante

10.

With a raggy feel

11.

Andante con moto

12.

Poco lento

Risoluto

13.

Comodo

14.

Melodic Dictation: QUIZ NO. 1

Piacevole

1.

Ritmico

2.

Amaroso

3.

Allegro vivace

4.

Serioso

5.

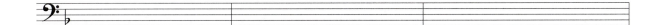

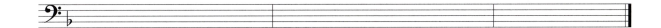

Melodic Dictation: QUIZ NO. 2

Grazioso

1.

Moderato

2.

Moderato

3.

Scorrevole

4.

Tempo di valse

5.

Harmonic Dictation: Extended and altered tertian harmony

1.
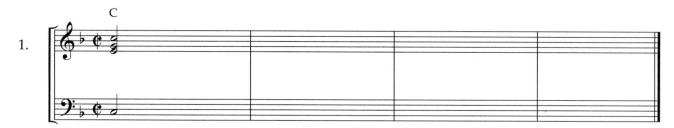

2.

3.

4.
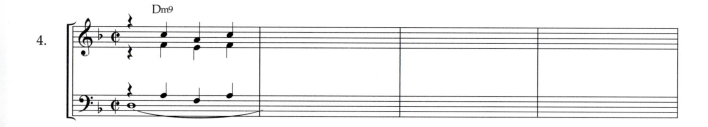

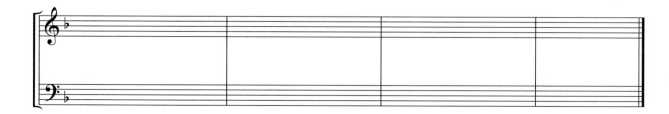

5.

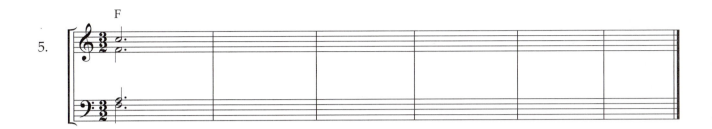

6.

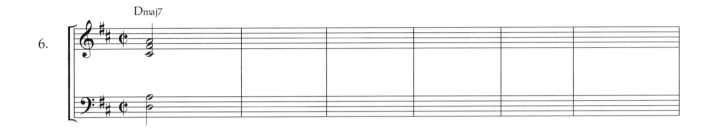

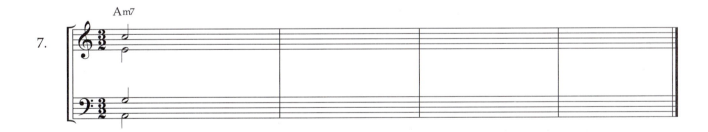

7.

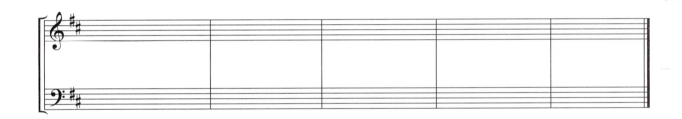

8.

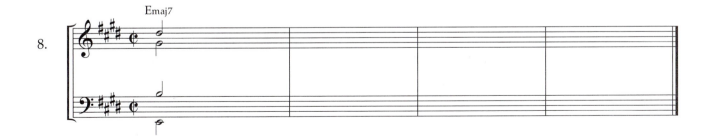

9.
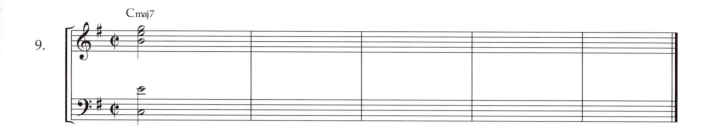

10.
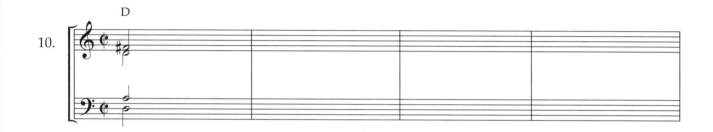

11.
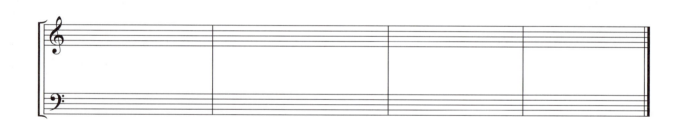

12.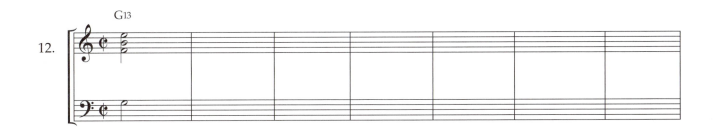

13.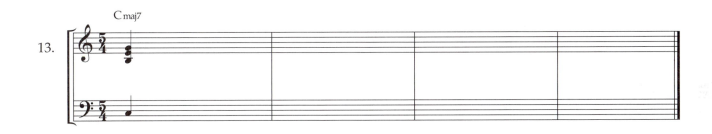

14.

Harmonic Dictation: QUIZ NO. 1

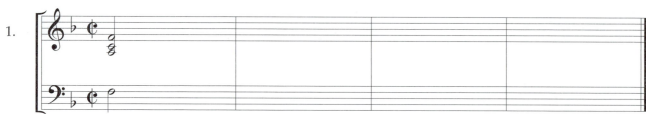

1.

2.

3.

4.

5.

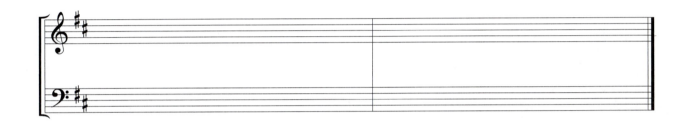

Harmonic Dictation: QUIZ NO. 2

1.
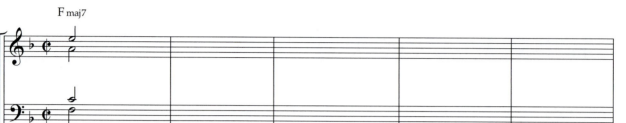

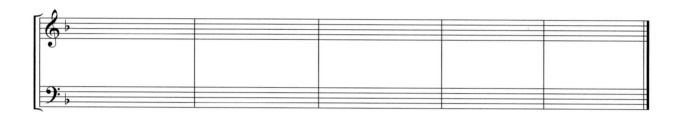

2.
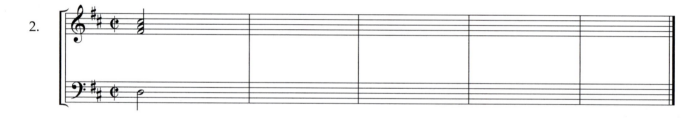

3.

4.

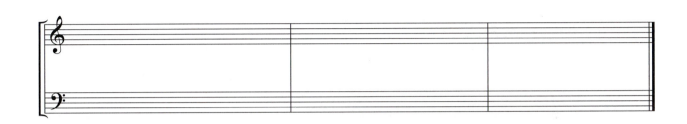

5.

Unit 21

Melodic Dictation: Exotic scales

1.

2.

3.

4.

Moderato

5.

Lugubre

6.

Allegretto

7.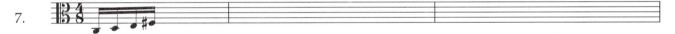

Lentement

8.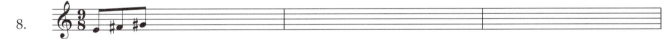

Class: _____

Name: _____

Professor: _____

Misterioso

9.

Gracieux

10.

Melancholique

11.

Moderato

12.

Gracioso

13.

Con spirito

14.

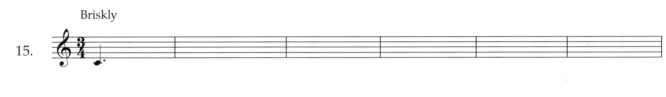

Briskly

15.

Pensivo

16.

Semplice

17.

18.

Furious

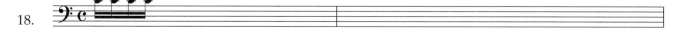

19.

Very slowly and sinuously

Name: _____

Melodic Dictation: QUIZ NO. 1

Andantino

1.

Vif

2.

Moderato

3.

Im Volkston

4.

Andante tenebroso

5.

Melodic Dictation: QUIZ NO. 2

Marcato

1.

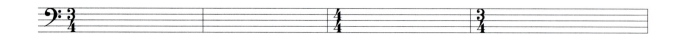

Doucement

2.

Semplice

3.

Con espressione

4.

Con forza

5.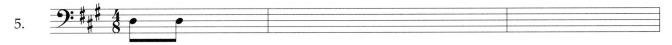

Part Music Dictation: Exotic scales

Modéré

1.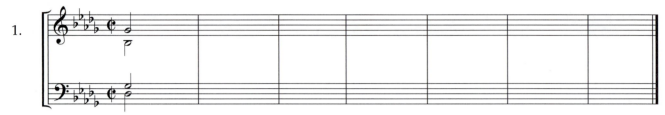

Lento

2.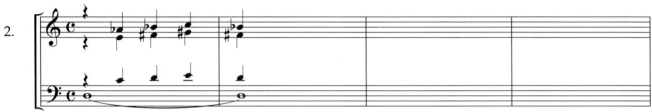

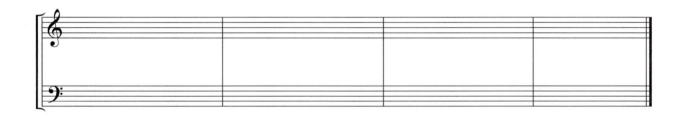

Grazioso

3.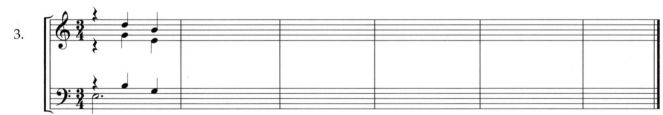

4. Assez lentement
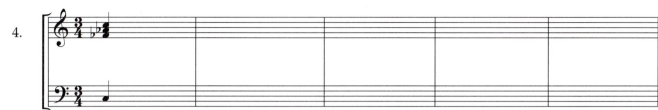

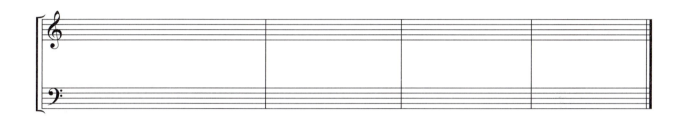

5. Comodo

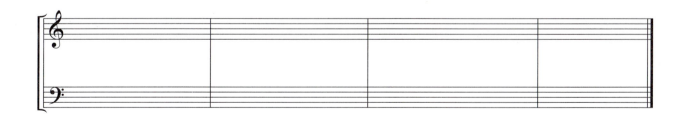

6.

Furioso

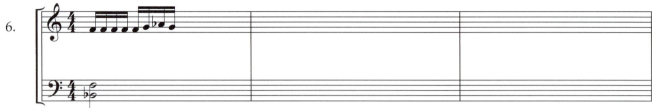

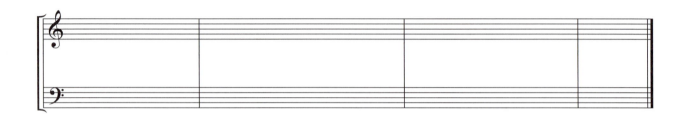

7.

Semplice

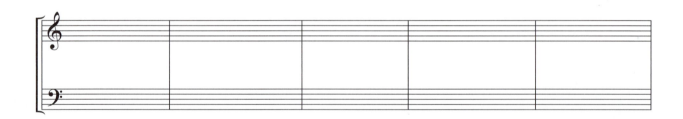

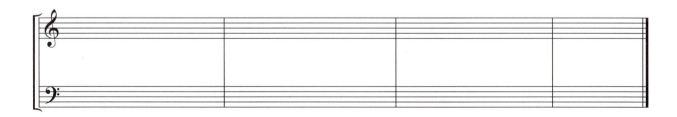

Adagio

8.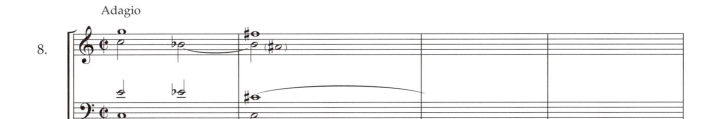

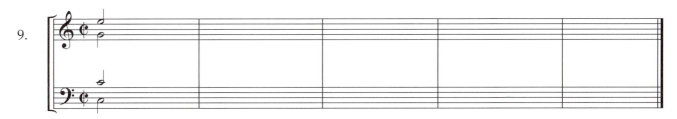

Chorale

9.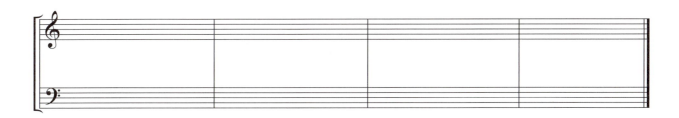

Allegro moderato

10.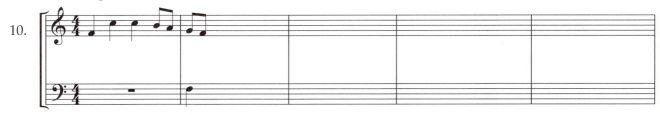

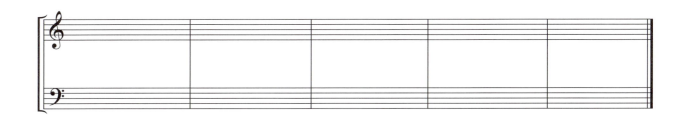

Part Music Dictation: QUIZ NO. 1

1.
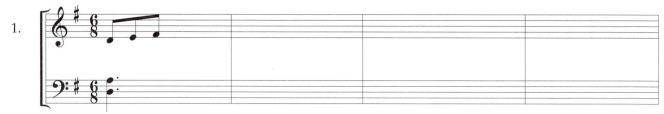

2.
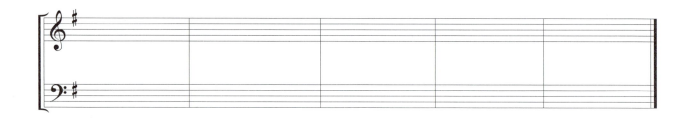

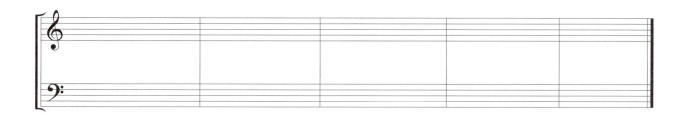

3.

Lebhaft

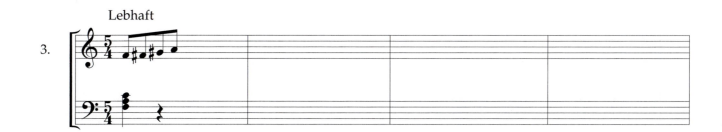

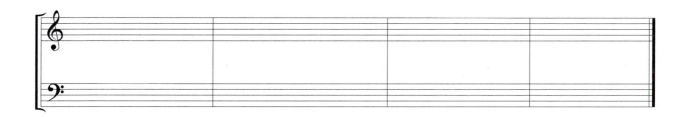

Part Music Dictation: QUIZ NO. 2

Scherzando

1.

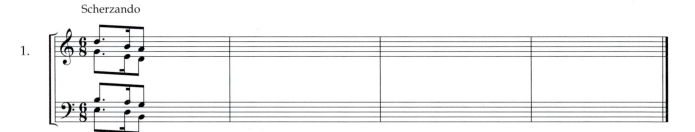

Moderato

2.

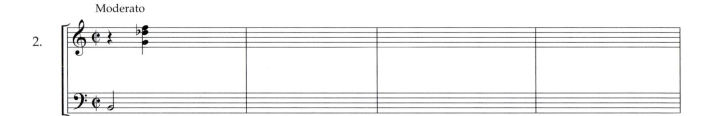

Tempo di Valse

3.

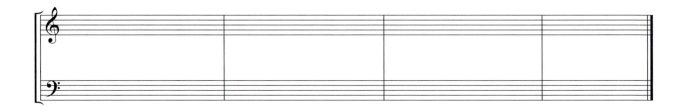

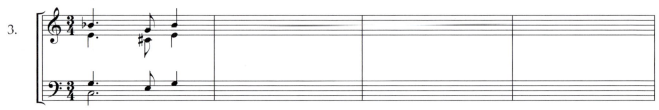

Unit 22

Melodic Dictation: Quartal harmony

Nicht zu schnell

1.

Feierlich

2.

Sehr langsam

3.

Fanfaro

4.

5. Lento

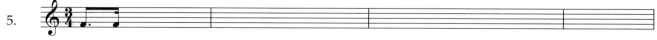

6. Grazioso

7. Lebhaft

8. Gondellied

Con fuoco

9.

Con forza

10.

Con tristezza

11.

Intenso

12.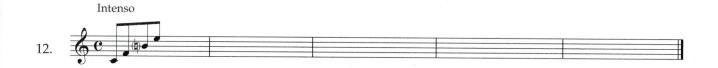

Allegretto

13.

Maestoso

14.

Langsam aber nicht schleppend

15.

Melodic Dictation: QUIZ NO. 1

Zart

1.

Lebhaft

2.

Gesangvoll

3.

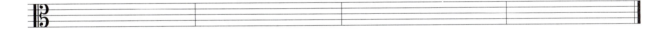

Vivace

4.

Melancholique

5.

Melodic Dictation: QUIZ NO. 2

Con moto

1.

Commodo

2.

Pesante

3.

Scherzando

4.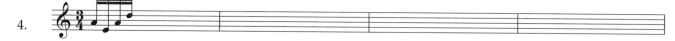

Giocoso

5.

Part Music Dictation: Quartal harmony

1.

Solenne

2.

Semplice

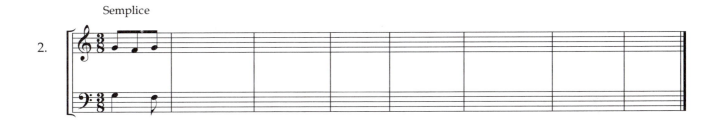

3.

Lullaby

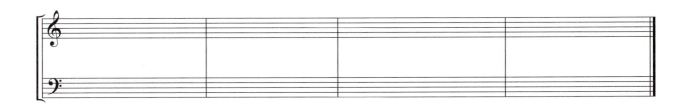

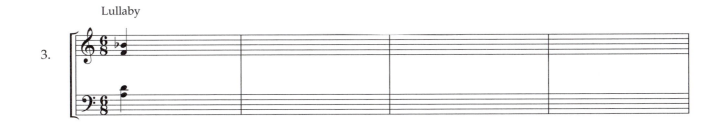

4.

Etwas langsam

5.

Allegretto

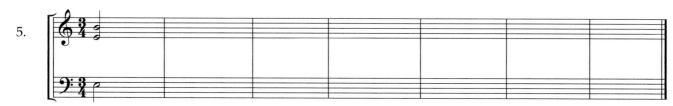

6.

Chorale

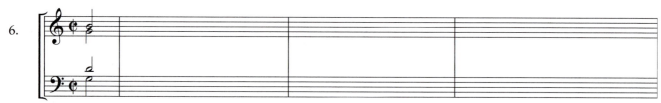

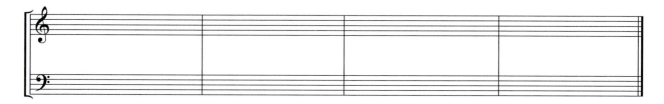

7.

Moderato

Stately

8.

Molto sostenuto

9.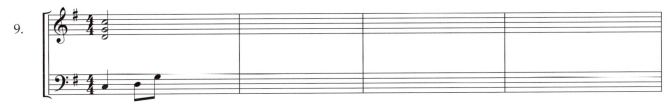

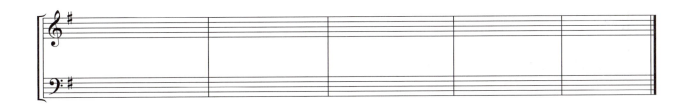

Breit

10.

Part Music Dictation: QUIZ NO. 1

Lento

1.

Maestoso

2.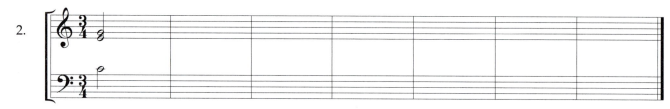

Comodo

3.

Larghetto

4.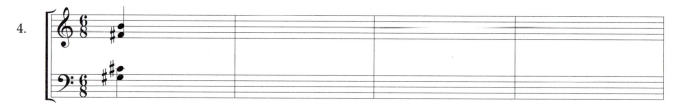

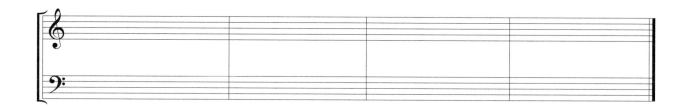

Maestoso

5.

Part Music Dictation: QUIZ NO. 2

Moderato

1.

Con moto

2.

Andantino

3.

Amabile

4.
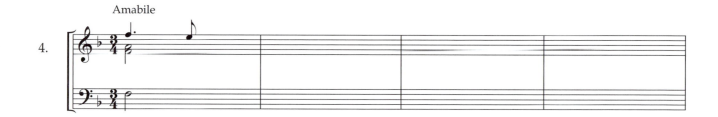

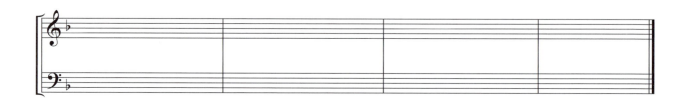

5.

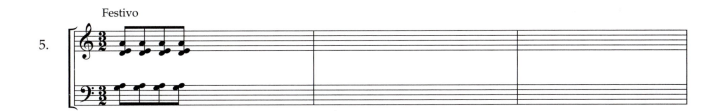

Unit 23

Part Music Dictation: Polyharmony and polytonality

1.

Allegretto

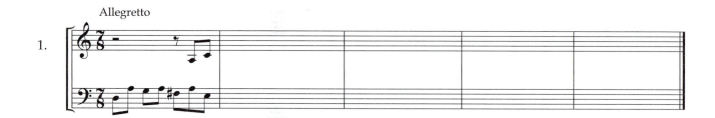

2.

Presto

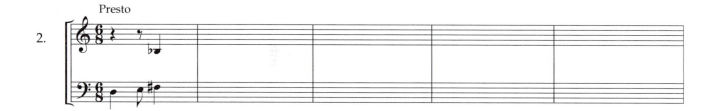

3.

Con forza

Class:

Name: _____

Professor:

Commodo

4.
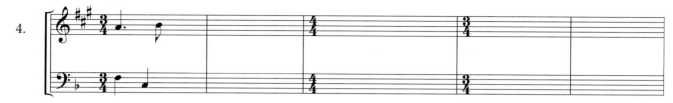

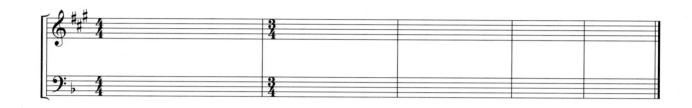

Sustained

5.

6.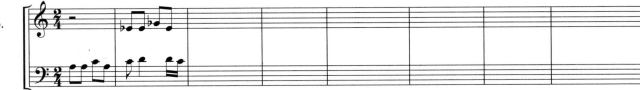

Semplice

7. Allegro

Maestoso

8.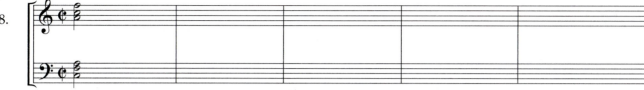

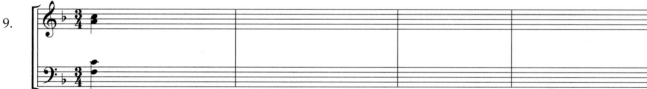

Rakishly

9.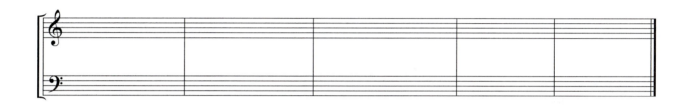

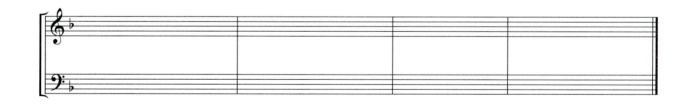

10.
Allegro giocoso

11.
Lentemente

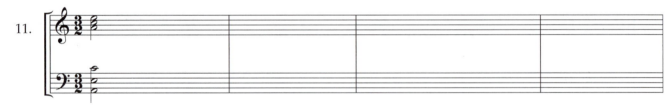

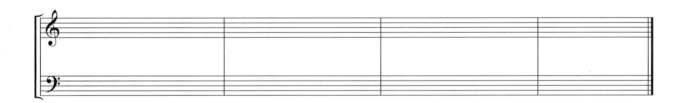

12.

Vigoroso

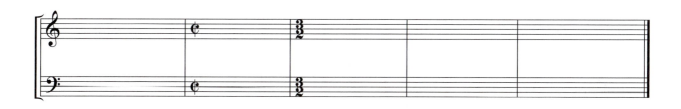

13.

Nostalgico

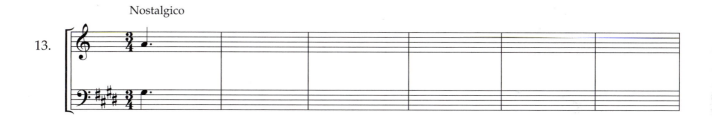

14.

Fanfare

Part Music Dictation: QUIZ NO. 1

1.

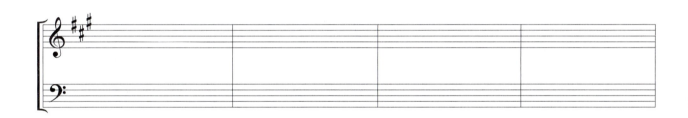

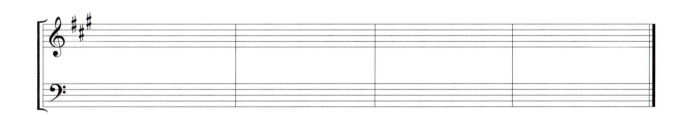

Grave

2.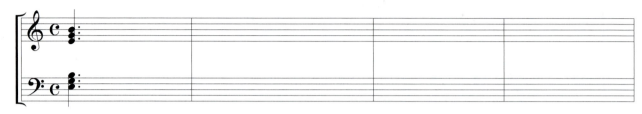

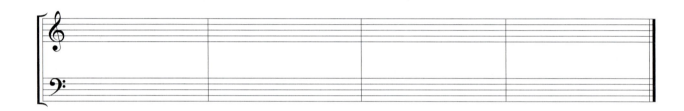

Allegro ma no troppo

3.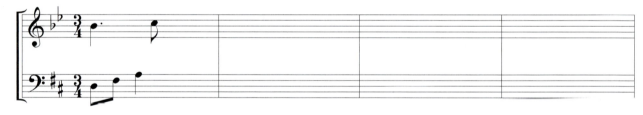

Vivace

4.

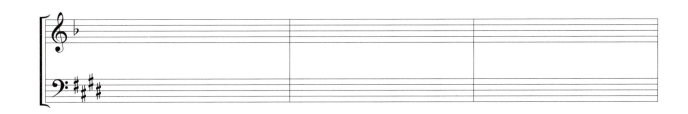

Allegretto

5.

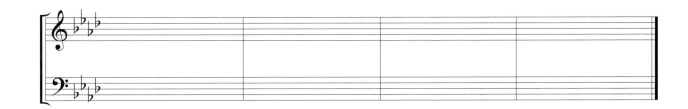

Part Music Dictation: QUIZ NO. 2

1.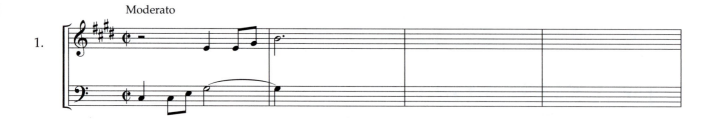

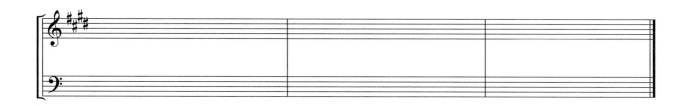

2.

3. Maestoso

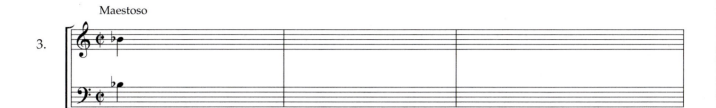

4. Doloroso

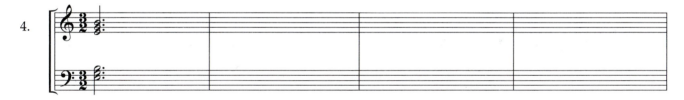

5.

Majestically

Unit 24

Melodic Dictation: Interval music

Preliminary Exercises

1.

2.

3.

4.

5.

6.

7.

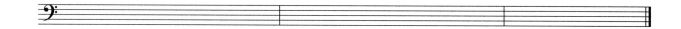

8.

9.

10.

Melodies

1.

2.

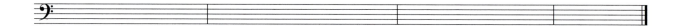

3.

4.

5. Alla Marcia

6. Massig

7. Assez vite

8. Feierlich

9. Andantino

10. Agitato

11. Deliberamente

12. Molto con brio

Scherzando

13.

Sinuously

14.

Name: _____

Melodic Dictation: QUIZ NO. 1

Lento

1.

Lullaby

2.

Heftig

3.

Allegro ma non troppo

4.

Lugubre

5.

Melodic Dictation: QUIZ NO. 2

Scherzando

1.

Larghetto

2.

Strepitoso

3.

Agitato

4.

Moderato

5.

Unit 25

Melodic Dictation: Serial music

1. Scherzando

2. Schleppend

3. Avec mouvement

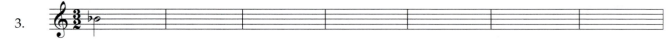

4. Giocoso

5. Con forza

6. Sinuously

7. Moderato

8. Freely

9. Animato

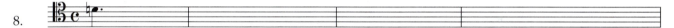

Molto lento e calmo

10.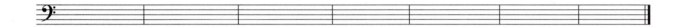

Heftig

11.

Deliberamente

12.

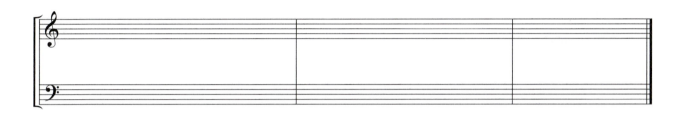

Melodic Dictation: QUIZ NO. 1

1. Fliessend

2. Allegro

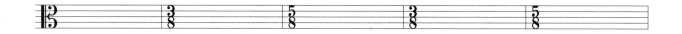

3. Con espressione

Melodic Dictation: QUIZ NO. 2

Con moto

1.

Andantino

2.

Mässig

3.